WORKING IT OUT

WORKING IT OUT

A Journey of Love, Loss,
and Hope

with a Foreword by Shay Sorrells

ABBY RIKE

New York   Boston   Nashville

FaithWords
Hachette Book Group
237 Park Avenue
New York, NY 10017

www.faithwords.com

Printed in the United States of America

First Edition: May 2011
10 9 8 7 6 5 4 3 2 1

FaithWords is a division of Hachette Book Group, Inc.
The FaithWords name and logo are trademarks of Hachette Book Group, Inc.

The publisher is not responsible for websites (or their content) that are not owned by the publisher.

Library of Congress Cataloging-in-Publication Data

Rike, Abby.
    Working it out : a journey of love, loss, and hope / Abby Rike.—1st ed.
    p. cm.
    ISBN 978-0-446-57503-4
    1. Rike, Abby.   2. Weight loss—United States—Case studies.
3. *Biggest Loser* (Television program)   4. Overweight women—United States—Biography.   5. Obesity—Psychological aspects—Case studies.
6. Grief in women—United States—Case studies.   7. Bereavement—United States—Case studies.   8. Husbands—Death—Psychological aspects—Case studies.   9. Children—Death—Psychological aspects—Case studies.   10. Faith—Case studies.   I. Title.
    RM222.2.R535 2011
    362.196'3980092—dc22
    [B]

    2010043417

In honor of Rick, Macy, and Caleb . . . may you impact others as you did me.

CONTENTS

Contents

FOREWORD

I 'm fine." A simple phrase with deeply buried meaning behind it. More often than not, those words are spoken by a person who is far from "fine"—but a person who is struggling to survive and yet appears to have it all together. I know the struggle behind those words all too well, after all I began building a wall of defenses against the world from an early age. Born to a heroin-addicted mother, I practically began life in survival mode. By the time I was five years old, I had witnessed my mother jumping from moving cars, being beaten to near death, and even selling her body for drugs. Eventually I ended up in and out of foster homes, suffering abuse at the hands of strangers. As my life progressed, I continued to feel void of meaning and I just...existed. This existence left me burying all my problems with any food I could get to my face. I had to reach nearly five hundred pounds before deciding that I wanted to find a way to live and not just survive. I arrived on *The Biggest Loser* ranch with huge empty spaces in my life. Little did I know, I'd be brought back to life by a woman with her own voids to fill.

I can tell you that only God could have known what He was doing when He put the two of us together. Abby Rike and I are about as opposite as opposites can be when it comes to upbringing and lifestyles. From the very first moment, however, it felt as if we were connected. As Abby said, "We are sisters. We just didn't know it." As room-mates during *The Biggest Loser* process, we stayed up having late-night talks like preteens at a slumber party—every night. Abby told me all about her beautiful family—Rick, Macy, and Caleb, and I told her all about my momma, Tammy. We cried, we laughed, and we were silent in those moments when no words could express the pain we both felt. Our tragedies were so different, mine built up over a lifetime and hers all commencing in one fell swoop, yet they bound us together and sealed our friendship. Abby is only a few years older than me, but she gave me such a protective and unconditional love, something like that of a mother. And I let her, which was something I had never done. I think during that time, as our bodies were shrinking, our hearts were expanding. Those gaping holes that we came with were being healed. Mind you, they will never be gone, but somehow our friendship gave them a new shape.

It makes my heart so happy to know that Abby has this opportunity to share her story with you. As you begin to read this story, you, too, will find so much more than just a tragedy that ends in triumph. If you are anything like I was, you ask yourself, "Will I ever get through this?" If you are ready, you may find some answers in these pages. Abby is inspiringly honest and joyfully candid about her story, and she genuinely wants to tell her story so that it may help as many people as possible. It is always good for the soul to know that there is someone else out there who has been where you are. This book will not only take you through the depths in order to understand just how deep grief can go, it also will take you to the highest pinnacle as you journey with Abby into her present day where she inspires others and continues to stand strong in her faith.

As a professional social worker I work with many clients who are in the midst of grief. From my personal experience I recognize that it is difficult to see the other side when you are in the thick of things. Abby Rike knows firsthand how lonely grief and loss can be and how devastating it is to our fragile hearts. Her story beautifully illustrates the amazing truth that no matter what life throws your way, no matter how painful or overwhelming, no matter how long you've been buried under the circumstances of your life, you can one day be much better than "fine." Abby's story confirms for us that there *is* always hope.

Shay Sorrells, MSW
The Biggest Loser, Season 8

WORKING IT OUT

CHAPTER I

Into the Depths

He who learns must suffer. And even in our sleep pain that cannot forget falls drop by drop upon the heart, and in our despair, against our own will, comes wisdom to us by the awful grace of God.

—Aeschylus

I am standing on the side of the road. It's as though my feet are planted in the ground, planted in cement. And I'm just waiting. No one will tell me anything. The dreadful scene that lies around the curve ahead remains a mystery for now as I'm frozen in place, standing like a statue at the defining moment of my life—eerily controlled while the life and love I'd cherished slips from my grasp. The intense combination of the red, white, and blue lights from the multitude of emergency vehicles penetrates my vision so severely I am overwhelmed by the visual assault. These are the lights that embody emergency, rescue, and often tragedy. Only this tragedy—my tragedy—has left us with no one to rescue.

My heart beats as if it wants out of my body, as if my heart knows it belongs in the van with the three people who had filled it with the joy of a truly perfect love. I ask the unavoidable question piercing my soul: "Is there a white van in the wreck?"

"Possible family member" is the emergency responder's reply into his radio.

"I need to know if there's a white van!"

And then simply, "Yes."

Friday, October 13, 2006, began as a calm and quiet day of precious hours shared between a mother and her brand-new, beautiful baby. And I knew beauty. I had watched it grow and radiate from every part of my daughter, Macy, for almost six years. I had witnessed the beauty of her innocence and the gift of her vivacious spirit. And now we'd been blessed once again with our blond-haired, blue-eyed, nine-and-a-half-pound perfect baby boy. The past eighteen days spent with Caleb had been absolute bliss. Caleb represented our hope for the future, and Rick and I savored the joy he added to our lives.

He was the only boy, Mommy's handsome "feller" (as I so lovingly called him), PaPa's fishing buddy, Daddy's little Longhorn, and the most wonderful completion of our family.

In those moments with my new family of four, I was acutely aware of the blessings that had been showered upon me. Not once did I take what I'd been given for granted;

they were my purpose, my joy, my truth, and my everything. My roles as wife and mother were everything I'd ever wanted, and I would not have traded lives with another human on the planet.

That particular Friday I wasn't feeling well. Aside from the normal fatigue every new mother faces, my chest felt unusually tight, and I was running a low-grade fever. Nevertheless, I wasn't too ill to miss time with my delightful son. With my husband Rick, a teacher, and Macy at school for the day, I had time alone with Caleb to play and treasure those fleeting moments of a child's infancy. Sitting on my bed with him in my lap, his head at my feet, I talked to him and cuddled him as we studied each other to our hearts' content.

When Macy and Rick eventually came in from school, I was immediately captured by Macy's excitement over what she described as the best day of her life. As part of fire safety week at school, she had climbed onto a fire truck and embraced that occasion with the unbridled zest for life she brought to every experience. She went on to tell us about a sweet little boy named Mcguire who wasn't in her class but had made her feel special by knowing her name. As I watched her trademark red curls dancing around her jovial face, she ran off to draw a picture of herself and Mcguire each wearing a crown, poised in a whimsical carriage.

Meanwhile, Rick and I discussed whether some of the symptoms I was having warranted a visit to the emergency room. Deciding I should go—better safe than sorry—we agreed that we didn't want Caleb exposed to any potentially harmful germs lurking in an ER waiting area. Rick would take him, Macy, and our two nieces, Madelyn and Maryl, to an open gym while I sought medical attention. I kissed Caleb and then Macy. I walked over to Rick standing behind our counter and kissed him, then went out to the car. Darting out from the house, Macy ran toward me as I was about to leave. From the car I called out, "Baby girl, you have got to get back in the house. You cannot just run out of the house!"

She replied, "I just wanted one more hug."

And then she stood in front of the car, wrapped her arms around herself, hugged herself, and said, "I love you!" I watched that exceptional child run back into the house, then pulled out of the driveway.

I'm at the emergency room and of course there's a long line. My name has been on the waiting list for almost an hour. I determine that my family—my life—headed in the opposite direction on their fun outing together, have surely arrived by now. I call Rick to check in and to my surprise he doesn't pick up. Weird. He always answers his phone. I call back. It rings and rings and rings. Voice mail. I call again. It rings and rings and rings. Voice mail. I know that more than enough time has passed for him to have arrived at the open gym, so I place a call to my ex-sister-in-law's house, where Rick was to pick up our nieces. I get right to the point. "What time did Rick pick up the girls?"

"He hasn't picked them up. I just went ahead and took Madelyn and Maryl."

And the feeling that something is horribly wrong begins to rise up from the pit of my stomach. Every fiber of my being knows that there's been a wreck. What I don't know is how bad it is.

I'm not completely conscious of my legs as they carry me to the front desk of the emergency room to explain that something has happened to my family. But somehow my body successfully reaches my car and I'm driving—fast. I'm driving and crying and praying out loud. "Please put angels all around my family. Please. All around them."

Five miles past our house, on the two-lane highway we've traveled so many times as a family, the sun begins to go down in the sky and a barrage of flashing lights comes into view.

Please put angels all around my family.

The onslaught of lights is almost too much, as I recognize the telltale signs that something truly terrible has occurred. I watch as uniformed officers redirect traffic around the blockades they have positioned, but I will not be redirected.

Please. All around them.

I pull over to an open space and get out of the car, standing there with my emergency room bracelet on. The frantic words escape my mouth. "I need to know if there's a white van!" I hear the "Yes" in reply. *But my life is in that van. My life is in that van.* Panic-stricken, I turn to the man beside me and ask, "Is it bad?" No one will make eye contact with me as the lights continue to flash and engulf my senses. The curt answer I am met with barely registers.

"Well, both of the cars caught on fire."

WHAT?! And I see the fire trucks, but no one will tell me anything. I call my mother who is on a trip with my father in Florida with the Trinity Valley College board of directors. I cry out with a torrent of incomprehensible explanations of the events unfolding before my eyes.

Approaching me from a distance, two stone-faced officers are coming with the news. I am vaguely aware of the phone still at my ear when each officer takes one of my arms. And from the mouth of a wonderful man named Officer Clint Pirtle—the only man to make eye contact with me—came the most horrific statement ever to reach my ears: "I'm so sorry. We found no survivors."

I drop to my knees, only to get right back up and plead, "Well, I need you to keep looking!" *Surely they just haven't found everybody yet.* And then I remember the phone in my hand. "Mother, he said they're all gone. He said they're all gone."

As Officer Pirtle takes the phone from my hands, I am left with the wave of numbness that has begun to infiltrate my body and mind. I instantly know Officer Pirtle's words are true; I know that they are gone. I know that I will never see them again. Without the benefit of denial, I'm left on the side of the road with only myself—truly broken, violently severed from the life I'd known only hours earlier. And just as if a limb has been severed from my body, shock takes over quickly, and I don't feel the pain right away. As I absorb that everything precious to me is gone, my mind becomes flooded with the knowledge that I have nowhere to go, no one to call, and nowhere to be.

Sitting on the back of an ambulance beside a young paramedic, I think back to that frantic drive toward the unimaginable place in which I now find myself. *I prayed that God would put angels all around my family. I just didn't mean this way.* I turn to the unassuming paramedic and am overcome with the urge to tell him our story. I tell him, with an eerie calmness, as though I haven't just been told that every member of my family is dead, "I have to tell you how wonderful my family was."

And as I explain that I'd had the most perfect husband, and the most perfect five-year-old daughter, and the most perfect two-week-old son, that precious man stands there and listens. I wonder aloud, "How could this be real when they were just going to open gym?"

And that wonderful man, a complete stranger, stands there and listens. A female paramedic joins us only to leave minutes later, unable to handle the words I feel compelled to share. But he never leaves; he stands quietly, offering no inane platitudes meant to comfort me.

As my ex-sister-in-law arrives on the scene and I get into her car, I am starkly aware of my complete solitude. I recognize the face of Ronnie Daniel, justice of the peace and the man here to fulfill the unimaginable duty of declaring my family dead. He comes to me and says, "Abby, I'm so sorry. If I could take their place I would." And he means it. He truly means it. "Is there anyone I can call?"

No, I think. *I don't have anybody to call. It's just me. My parents are on their trip in Florida; my brother is at a football game in Georgia; and my husband's not answering.*

I leave the scene with my ex-sister-in-law and head to my house—our home—to pack some things. I have no reservations about returning to the house we shared as a family. It is truly a home in every sense of the word: a place of safety, love, and comfort. It is the happiest place on earth to me. As I enter the house, I am greeted by balloons saying "It's a Boy!" I pass Caleb's stroller in the living room and walk into our bedroom, robotically filling a bag. My face is strangely dry; I am without tears. I walk out the door into an existence I cannot comprehend. Just like that, at one fell swoop, I know that I'm no longer a wife to the most amazing man I'd ever met. No longer a mother to the two most precious children in the world. *Where do I go? What now?*

CHAPTER 2

A Light in the Dark

By His light I walked through darkness.

—Job 29:3

I n the days following the wreck, no one could understand how I was doing so well. No one could understand why I was not crazy. No one really knew what to expect, but they came anyway. The amount of support from the people of our community was extremely comforting, and to see the multitude of lives Rick and my family had touched brought consolation. But as my mind digested the reality of the wreck, I knew all eyes were on me. I decided very early on that I would never be anyone's stumbling block. I was going to be an example to our beloved students. After the accident, I had to take an immediate assessment of my beliefs and ask, *Do I really believe what I think I believe?* And the answer I always came back to was a definite *Yes. I do.*

Those who came to sit beside me that night said that I looked different, that I was almost glowing. It was as if God had laid a blanket of peace over my shattered heart. And I knew that this was a pivotal point in my life. It is easy to have faith and proclaim your love for the Lord when you have a perfect life—very easy. And people will sometimes dismiss you. But it's an entirely different thing when those beliefs remain the same through a tragedy beyond anything people can imagine. I had always been very grounded in my faith, but never had God's love for me been so tangible. I was a living example of the concept of a peace that passes all understanding. I should have been catatonic; I should have been prostrate in despair and never gotten up after this. But because of God's grace I did. God's grace was and is sufficient.

A few days after I buried my husband and two children, the humanness of grief hit. I went for a walk outside, attempting to clear my head of the overwhelming emptiness I felt. I was completely alone and heartbroken as I walked around my parents' backyard under the shade of an oak tree. The Glad Oak (as my mother had always called it) was the site where Rick and I vowed to love each other forever—where our two lives were ceremonially joined as one. Three years earlier Rick, Macy, and I stood beneath that very oak and promised that only death would ever separate us. With silent tears I paced the acres of my parents' land, calling out to God. "Lord, what do I do? What do You want me to do with my life? I'm open. I'm willing. What do I do? Help me."

Suddenly, two little yellow butterflies caught my eye. They emerged seemingly out of nowhere, and I watched as they flew, playing and dancing around each other, fluttering freely in the air with a childlike grace. Struck by their beauty, I looked on as a huge orange monarch butterfly lovingly swooped down over them. It soared directly toward me and flew in a circle around my body, swaddling me in a blanket of warmth, then coming to land inches from my feet. The ethereal creatures stayed only moments, but they left me with a powerful, overwhelming sense of peace. And I knew without a shadow of a doubt that I'd been given the gift I so desperately needed. My family was together, their souls transcending death, and they were okay. *Just as I will also be okay again one day.* And I expressed my gratitude to God. *Thank You for caring enough to send a broken soul a little glimmer of hope.*

The people that made me a better me are gone. What now? What do I do now?

What plan does God have for me? If I have to suffer like this, then I want my life to matter. I want to know what I'm supposed to do. I want to know my plan. I am shattered and I'm trusting with childlike faith that God will put me back together again. This loss cannot be for naught.

—Abby Rike, written December 3, 2006, 1:00 a.m.

PART ONE

The Caterpillar Stage

CHAPTER 3

Boy Meets Girl

A soulmate is someone who has locks that fit our keys, and keys to fit our locks...Each unveils the best part of the other. No matter what else goes wrong around us, with that one person we're safe in our own paradise. Our soulmate is someone who shares our deepest longings, our sense of direction. When we're two balloons, and together our direction is up, chances are we've found the right person. Our soulmate is the one who makes life come to life.

—*Richard Bach*

In January 2003, I was at a speech tournament with my team of students. I was a coach for the University Interscholastic League speaking program at Canton High School. UIL is a program unique to Texas schools that encompasses athletics, music, and academics—all separate entities with which we serve the students in our schools. The program's competitive events give students the little something extra they so desperately need. In the academics arena, students can choose from among thirty-two different events, including spelling, mathematics, computer science, history, and more. My job was to oversee all the speaking events: prose and poetry interpretation, persuasive and informative speaking, Lincoln-Douglas and cross-examination debate, and the one-act play—a huge undertaking for me but absolutely worth it.

In the coach's lounge at the tournament, I noticed a tall man with masculine features and glasses, dressed in a suit, and I was suddenly aware of my own denim capris, black tank top, and sweater. As the coaches began talking, I soon met him and learned that his name was Rick Rike, and he was the UIL coordinator at Aubrey High School, a 2-A school a few hours from Canton, a 3-A school. In Texas, schools are classified according to their student population. Divisions range from the smallest 1-A school to the largest 5-A school. Our students had never competed against each other except at practice tournaments, but they were very strong and tremendously competitive at all levels, something a little unusual for a 2-A school. As we continued to chat, we started talking about doing a clinic together with our students so that they could hear another judge's viewpoint on their performance. He gave me his home number, his cell, his school number, and his e-mail address. There surely would not be a problem getting in touch with one another!

Both of us remained really busy, not yet knowing what was in store for us; so, we e-mailed once or twice but nothing more. February brought about the cross-examination debate for my district. The head of the district hired Rick as a judge, inadvertently causing our paths to cross once again. After my top-seeded team suffered a loss and unjustifiably low speaker points, the students were out of the running for the next rounds. My second-seeded team members advanced to the next round, knowing they would more than likely be outmatched. Winning, under all the current circumstances, would be a long shot.

In a moment of mischief the students asked if they could have a little fun in the final round. I told them not to embarrass the school, themselves, or me but to go ahead and enjoy. Rick was judging this round at the last minute even though he had quite a long drive ahead of him back to Aubrey. My two students, who also happened to be huge Star Wars fans, inserted a hilarious comment about Chewbacca in their presentation, creating a great story and several giggles for the ride home. And in an unheard-of move, Rick voted for my team.

Later, reading his ballot from the event, I fixated on the section reserved for personal comments. I laughed aloud at the joke he'd written about now having to make the long trek back to Aubrey with his "invisible friend." I was instantly drawn to his sense of humor and intelligence. Looking over that ballot, and then over at my students, I said, "Kids, this is someone I could like."

Various events and different schedules kept us from running into each other again for a few months. And before I knew it, it was a Saturday in May and we were at the state meet. After the awards ceremony, during which one of my students took first place, Rick came to congratulate me and discuss plans to celebrate later that evening. He said he and his team were going to the Oasis outside of Austin on Lake Travis, so we decided to go along. The three students with me knew by now that I was interested in him, and they were in rare form. Those girls were like part of my family, and I lovingly warned them that they better be on their best behavior.

Rick and I happened to pull up to the restaurant with our cars facing each other and began walking in. Suddenly, I looked up and Rick was fifty paces ahead of me. *Man!* I thought, silently wishing we'd walked in and sat together. My group entered the restaurant and found no empty spots at Rick's table, but that didn't discourage me. I pulled up a chair, and we talked and laughed a bit before I went back to my table. "Girls," I said, "this is what it looks like when you've been dismissed! This is what it looks like when someone is not interested in you!" And we had a hearty laugh over the situation.

Rick's group talked about going to play mini golf, but I had already decided I was done putting myself out there. I shared my plans to take the girls to Sixth Street in Austin, just a fun place to walk around and visit quirky stores. On the way out of the restaurant, we stopped in an area where other students were mingling and dancing. The girls hung out a little before we left for Sixth Street, so as we walked out of the restaurant, I noticed we were leaving at the same time as Rick and his bunch. Rick was ahead of us and didn't know it, but we were watching him with his shirt over his head, doing a Beavis and Butt-head impersonation. Hearing our uncontrollable laughter, Rick discovered us watching him, and he turned beet red.

We took the opportunity to convince one of Rick's students to come with us to Sixth Street, and soon they all decided to join us. Once on Sixth Street, Rick and I finally started talking as we came to a coffee shop with an improv show. We sat down with our coffee. The girls were acting up like true teenagers, making it hard to concentrate on the intriguing man sitting beside me. I reminded them of the sacrifices I'd made over the past few months and asked for just one night of good behavior! They obliged, and I found myself enjoying every word that came out of Rick's mouth.

We caught a cab back to our hotel, leaving Rick and me to exchange the most awkward hug ever showcased in public. It was awkward to the point of almost painful! The ungainly display was compounded by my lovable but juvenile group's "Ooooooooooh" as I got into the cab—leaving Rick red-faced once again.

I told myself I was definitely getting an e-mail on Monday. Tuesday came, and I was still waiting for it. I swallowed every ounce of pride and e-mailed him; there was no denying the fact that I was really interested. It was perfectly clear to me why Rick was the most eligible bachelor in Aubrey. Not overly debonair or suave, he was just good to his core and everything that I could ever hope to have. I e-mailed a pretty benign message just saying I'd had fun at the state meet. Upon receipt of my e-mail, he realized that the e-mail he sent Monday never made it; there was a problem with his server. Replying to my e-mail, he also sent his original message. I was smitten and invited him to a community performance on Thursday of my play *The Cover of Life,* which had made it to the state meet. I was overjoyed when he accepted.

I soon found out that Rick had tickets to the Dallas Mavericks playoff game—game six—on the same night as the play. I immediately assumed that he'd be going to the game, and I genuinely told him that it was not a problem. I completely understood. Without hesitation, he expressed his desire to come to the play instead, and he affirmed what I knew to be true: When men are interested, they will make it happen.

Word traveled all around school that Rick was coming to the performance and that we'd be going to dinner at my favorite restaurant, Two Senoritas, after the play. It was a big deal for the students; they knew I didn't date. I made sure to inform them that they had better find another place to eat that night. Soon, it was Thursday; the play was over, and we were standing at Rick's car. Rick opened my door; on the seat was a bunch of spring flowers and a card.

Abby,

I just wanted to write you a quick note to say first and foremost congratulations on a wildly successful State Meet. As a fellow UIL coach, I fully appreciate how much that State pin means. I also appreciate how many hours went into reaching your goals . . . What a wonderful job you did with that crew. Enough now about the professional stuff! I want to thank you for the invitation out here to beautiful East Texas. I had such a good time hanging out and relaxing Saturday night and into Sunday in Austin. Thanks for allowing us to do fun stuff instead of putt-putt. ☺ *Ok . . . that is all I have to say for now because I am writing this at school and I need to get on the road so I am not late for the show!*

$$R^2$$

—*Rick Rike, written to Abby on their first date, see page 261*

In the restaurant that night, I never looked away from him. I was so focused. We talked and talked and talked, but back at my car, Rick gave me a hug and then drove off, abruptly ending a magical night.

Once home I couldn't shake the feeling that I didn't get enough time with him. I called him under the guise of wanting to make sure he'd found his way back to the highway. It worked. We talked as he drove the three hours back to Aubrey and still after he arrived at home, deciding to meet each other again Saturday at Maggiano's.

Dinner at Maggiano's was our second date, and I loved that he said, "I hear the portions are really big. Wanna split?" We were both teachers, and such a frugal suggestion was music to my ears. We then went to a sports bar, and he held my hand a little as we walked in. There were no awkward silences. He jokingly informed me of a theater job open at Aubrey High, and we laughed about it, both of us well aware that I was beyond happy at Canton High. The sports bar was becoming loud, and I was having a hard time listening. Captivated by our conversation, I asked if we could go somewhere to talk more easily.

At the Double Tree Hotel bar, he sat with his back to the Mavericks game so he wouldn't be distracted. Free-flowing conversation kept us from heading to my car before midnight. In the parking lot we noticed that security was not very happy with our loitering, and we were forced to leave without a first kiss. Another hug and we set the third date for Monday; I'd make dinner (despite my complete inability to cook!) and he'd meet Macy and my parents. Our courtship was going at warp speed, and it all felt completely natural.

On Monday afternoon, I took Macy over to my parents' house, then came back to start cooking. I put chicken in a skillet and discovered that unbeknownst to me, my stove was not working. What a glaring example of my lack of prowess in the kitchen! I called Rick to say we'd be going out—my treat, but we'd swing by my parents' house first for him to meet Macy. Having long ago resigned myself to the fact that no man was ever going to meet Macy, this was a huge step for me. But with Rick, there were so many people who knew and loved him in the community and at his job; it wasn't like bringing a stranger.

I watched that wonderful man meet my baby. As they ran off to play with her Play-Doh, I could feel the shift in my life. For so long, it had just been the two of us, Macy and me.

I was twenty-six years old, and pregnant. While my heart leaped for joy over the precious life growing within my body, my mind knew what needed to be done. I'd been married for almost four years, and it was not a good marriage—

certainly not a situation into which I'd ever bring my child. So I did what I had to do. Four months into the pregnancy, I left my husband in Houma, Louisiana, and returned home to Texas.

Six months away from being a single mother, I applied for jobs and was hired by Max Callahan, one of the greatest men on earth. He hired me even though I was four months pregnant, knowing he'd have to find substitutes and work around my maternity leave. He had seen one of my plays when I was a first-year teacher in Kemp, a small school in the same district as Canton, and he had never forgotten it. So he did what no one else would've done and offered me a job.

I didn't tell anyone that I was separated from my husband. I wore my wedding ring to school every day. But eventually, in a small town, when a husband is never around and no one ever sees him, people figure things out. People later learned I was getting a divorce, but they didn't know my story. In a small town, it's a big deal to be female, alone, pregnant, and divorced.

The day I found out I was having a girl, I was joyous. Busy with my work at school, soon it was fall and the time had come for her to arrive. I'd had back labor for almost thirty hours and wasn't dilating, so the doctor induced labor. The umbilical cord was dangerously close to the baby's head, and her heart rate was dropping with every contraction. She was in distress, and would be delivered via emergency C-section.

My mother was in the room with me, and she cried out immediately after seeing her granddaughter, "Oh, Abby!

She has red hair!" And I thought to myself, *Are you sure she's mine? How did I have a child with red hair?*

The moment I laid eyes on her, I was changed. Her head was absolutely perfect, and she was just beautiful. I remember walking to the nursery to see her, and she was just six and a half pounds and so small. She looked like a porcelain china doll. Perfect head, perfect smattering of red hair. Beside her were these cone-headed dark-haired babies. I felt sorry for the other babies to have Macy in the middle. I went so far as to tell the nurse I felt sorry for the parents. How could they come see their babies when they'd see Macy and think, *Oh, I wish she was mine!* I thought she was the most beautiful creature I'd ever seen in all my life. (Imagine my shock when Rick saw a newborn picture of Macy and made that "Oh, my" face that you make once the child is older and cuter.) Thank God for mother's eyes, eh?

Macy was different from the very beginning. At three days old, home from the hospital, she could hold her head up, perfectly erect. Her eyes never darted back and forth; they were stunningly bright and alert. That first night home, she followed the circle of a holiday wreath hanging on the wall, her eyes slowly tracing the curved outline—taking everything in.

As perfect as she was, nothing rocked my world as much as having her. She didn't sleep at night. She didn't nap. She was delightful, but she was needy. She was never spoiled, and I don't believe that you can spoil kids with love. But she was high maintenance in that she needed a lot of attention and stimulation. I could never sit her in a bouncer; she was not satisfied with that. If I needed to shower, I would put her tub in the shower with me. There was never a break.

She had colic and could never get comfortable. She lost weight in the beginning. I took her to get her picture taken, and when I looked at the proof, I saw that she looked blue around her mouth. I was the panicked mom who went to the pediatrician thinking something was wrong and they needed to fix her. My breast milk dried up almost instantly from the fear. I had to put her on Nutramigen, the champagne of baby formula, and that expense alone was formidable.

Aside from that, I was in the midst of a painful divorce. And let's face it. If the marriage is bad, then the divorce will not be fun. My divorce would not be finalized for two years. I refused to agree to unsupervised visitation until Macy turned three years old, the longest time a court would agree to. I was certainly not sending my newborn daughter into an environment I'd felt compelled to leave to protect her.

I went two years with no child support and didn't have enough money for both of us. So Macy had clothes. Macy had diapers. Macy had Nutramigen. And I made do. Not with a poor-pitiful-me attitude, but with the knowledge that I was providing for my daughter in the best way I could.

I wanted to be a good mom, and I was so nervous and exhausted, but I did the very best I could. I knew I was becoming a better person. It's really easy to be generous and caring when your needs are taken care of. And for the first time in my life my needs weren't taken care of. If there was ever a time when I needed to figure out who I was, it was that time. It was the first time I had ever loved something more than myself. And that's what motherhood is.

Macy did everything early and desired constant stimulation. She crawled at four and a half months old. She was pulling up by five and a half months and took her first step the day before she turned seven months. Macy was walking around by eight months and running at ten months. Her language development was just as advanced. She said her first word at six months: "Mom." She spoke in three-word sentences at a year old. By fifteen months she was having conversations. She was truly the most exceptionally gifted child. It is hard for people to believe unless they were there to see it.

I returned to work when Macy was six weeks old. She had a brief stint in day care for about two weeks, until I decided that I was going to quit my job before I took her there again. She was constantly sick, had allergies, and needed breathing treatments regularly. As soon as I'd get her back in the routine of sleeping in her own bed, she'd get sick again.

Finding Nanny Pat, a phenomenal woman with an English accent and a heart of gold, was one of the biggest blessings in my life. She is at the top of the list of people outside my family who have changed my life for the better. I trusted Nanny Pat implicitly because I didn't have to worry about Macy's welfare. I could tell by Macy's demeanor that she was being cared for and cherished. Knowing she was in such good care, I could concentrate on my tasks at work. In fact, Nanny Pat was much calmer with her than I was at times, and it was so wonderful for Macy to be around the calming influence of someone who so patiently and kindly cared for her. Nanny Pat never missed a day. She and her husband, Ronnie, loved Macy like their own, and you can't put a price on that.

My mother worked full time but kept Macy on most Saturdays. She and Macy were kindred spirits. Macy would clean house with her as she got older and they'd play in the Magic Room—a pink princess room with a pink crushed-velvet couch—the perfect place for childhood fantasy. That time spent together fostered a relationship both my mother and Macy treasured. It also made Macy feel that she didn't need just me. I believe one of the worst things a mother can do is nurture a child's anxiety by not stepping away so that the child can experience someone else. Macy had several different places to go where she felt at home. She was secure and well adjusted because she had such great caregivers.

I enjoyed Macy's infancy as much as I could. But I was a different person then, growing into the person I would become. I was a strict disciplinarian; I showered her with love, but I didn't put up with any tomfoolery. I certainly was not going to allow a nine-month-old to run things! Macy was strong willed and an absolute delight. I always knew she had my mother as the safe place to fall; I had to be a strong, consistent example for her. Still, I didn't have the martyr mentality that I could never leave my child or do anything for myself. A mother's priority must be her child;

they didn't ask to be born. As a single mother, I never had anyone to pass her off to, but once a month I'd go out to dinner with friends. Macy and I spent a lot of time at my parents' house after school. I never had to feel that I was imposing on anyone.

With every milestone she reached, she became more independent, which thrilled me. I was never a person who needed to be needed. I wanted to raise my children to leave the nest. It was my job to make sure that they'd be fine without me, and that they'd thrive on their own. I never would've thought I'd be learning to live without them.

At almost two years old, Macy was thriving, as was I. My professional life was just as on track as my home life. I'd had much success with my students at the speaking events, taking three of them to compete at the state level. I was having the most fulfilling year at school, watching the students grow as actors and actresses in a beautiful play. The chemistry of that particular group of kids was like nothing I'd ever experienced. They were so talented, and we were like family.

I was awarded Teacher of the Year in my third year at Canton High School and received the honor before a standing ovation. But it had been too long since I'd had a companion to share my successes with. I lived in a small town with no one to date, no one to meet, and the stigma of being a single mother everywhere I went. I prayed that God would send someone worthy of us and that I'd be worthy of him. I fervently prayed that we would meet someone. I prayed for Rick before I met him. There had to be more than just work and life as a single mother. I had always wanted a good marriage. There was something missing.

My prayers had been answered. The night Rick met Macy, a little over a week had passed since our first date. It never felt rushed, only natural, and good, and right. After dinner that night, we sat on my couch and talked until he got the nerve to initiate our first kiss. It was extremely awkward and absolutely perfect all at the same time. We talked and talked, as though mesmerized by each other's voices until we noticed it was 3:00 a.m. Rick, realizing he had to be at work in a few hours, remembered that he still had to drive the three hours back home. Arriving at work with little time to spare, Rick showered at the school and then worked a full day without rest. We simply couldn't be bothered with something as trivial as sleep when getting to know each other was so intriguing. While someone else might have complained of too much togetherness, I never once thought *I need a break from this man.* No matter how many hours we spent together, I wanted more.

We still hadn't had any uncomfortable conversations to define what we were; it just was. He never played games, and it didn't feel like we were moving too fast. We knew it was strange to some people, but to us it was just right.

Abby,
     Ok . . . so I'm not sure this is the most fitting card ever,
but I was kinda rushed, so I had to make do. It hardly seems

*possible we have only "known" each other since last Saturday,
but so be it. The one thing I am sure of in life is that I love
to have a good time...AND a good time I have had the past
week or so. Whenever we are not hanging out or spending time
together, I am constantly looking forward to the next time we
will see each other. You are one of the nicest, most intellectual,
honest, and REAL people I have ever had the good fortune
of knowing...I learn so much about you everytime we are
together. In this upcoming week we are going to learn so much
more about each other's friends and families. For some reason
that just seems natural...☺*

R^2

—Rick Rike to Abby, May 2003, see page 261

A few weeks into it, I knew that I loved him. I sat down
to write him a card saying just that. I certainly didn't plan
to give him the card. But I wanted to write down the exact
moment that I knew.

*Okay...so you've just left my house and it's 2:30 in the
morning...And I'm writing this knowing I won't give this to
you for quite some time...I guess what it boils down to is you
piqued my interest with the infamous "ballot." Then I had
the absolute BEST first date of my life on Thursday...two
weeks ago...I realized then that you were the kind of man
that I could love. I didn't think that would ever happen so that
was really exciting! Then we kept spending time together and
having all those incredible talks. And the more I know of you
the more I realize I am falling head over heels for you.*

I know people throw the love word around without much
thought to what that really means. I take it so very seriously.
Love is way more than a passing feeling. It's about mutual
respect and caring enough about someone else to put their needs
above your own . . . because you KNOW they want your
needs to be met as well. It is the place where you feel safe to be
yourself, and where you want to be regardless of the type of day
you've had. Love is patient, kind, not jealous or boastful . . .
Using this as my standard, then without hesitation I can tell
you that I love you.

You talk about not knowing if there's one perfect person
for everyone, and now I believe there is. I think God
created you for me and me for you. You surpass my wildest
fantasies. I think we complement each other so well. It just
works! We just "get" it. I know it's insane to feel this way
after two and a half weeks, but there it is. I'm in it . . . in it
completely.

—*Abby to Rick on May 22, 2003, see page 262*

It was my turn to plan the date, so we went for Italian
food and brought it to my friend Julie's log cabin to have
dinner on the patio. After dinner, he moved to a chair and
began talking about one of his good friends who was supposed to have come out the week before to meet me. Rick
was upset, saying she knew how much it meant to him for
her to meet me. He slipped, "She knows that I . . ." And
stopped. I immediately knew it—I could sense it. *He loves
me!* He looked at me like a deer in headlights as I strolled
over to him and sat on his lap. "She knows that you what?"

He tried to avoid the question. "She knows that you what?" And he told me. "That I love you."

My response was instantaneous: "I love you! And I have a card that says that I love you. And it's not just because of this. I wrote it before this!" We sat in blissful oblivion, soaking up the life-altering words we'd just shared, as a FedEx truck pulled up—in the rain in the middle of the night. Rick laughed at the bizarre occurrence, but I was too captivated by our exchange to pay much attention to the interruption.

Our relationship progressed quickly. Summer was here, and Rick had already planned to go to New York. So we decided that we'd go to New York together in July. We went on several dates with Macy, and once in a while, he stayed over at my house in the guest bedroom.

One day, he told me that the job at Aubrey High had come open again and asked if I'd be interested in taking it. At this point, the job had come open three times, and I needed to give it serious consideration. This time it was right. My head spun as I realized, *I'm going to quit my job and change schools to be with Rick.* I knew it was a huge step for Macy and me, but also a wonderful expression of how much I loved him and how committed I was to a life with him.

I went to my parents to tell them the news. "I'm quitting my job and taking the position at Aubrey High School. Macy and I are moving." They knew how serious I was about Rick as well as liking and respecting him from what they knew firsthand, and my parents voiced their approval.

With their support and encouragement, the next step was to visit my principal at Canton, Max Callahan, to tell him that I was resigning. He was not happy. "You're kidding me," was his incredulous response. I replied with conviction. "I'm not. I've met someone. I've met someone who I love, who loves Macy, and is a wonderful person."

Despite my spirited avowal, Max was less than thrilled, but his response revealed his admirable character. "Okay, Abby. I want you to be happy."

With the support of those closest to me and the highest hopes, I'd decided to embark on a new chapter of my life.

Abby,

I saw this card the other day and it just seemed to fit. Indeed you have done it. You decided to move to Aubrey, you told your folks, you told Mr. C and now you put your house on the market... WOW! You have done it and are doing it... MOVING TO AUBREY! I am so excited and so sure this is the right thing to do that it is almost scary. The prospect of you and Macy moving here once seemed very far-fetched. Now, we are going house shopping Friday! What the heck? I am reminded every day just how lucky I am to have found someone as beautiful, intelligent, kind, and loving as you... AND you get me! Did I mention how great it is that you get me??

The coming days, weeks, months, and YEARS of late-night talks, family gatherings, UIL tournaments, in-service days, summer trips to fun places, long days at home, and Macy games/cheer camps, and school milestones are truly exciting to me. (It is never too early for us to begin work on her Valedictorian Address for the Class of 2019.☺)

I do so love you, Abby Davis. The incredible leap of faith you are taking right now obviously affirms to me just how much you love me as well. We have talked about this being more than just an Abby and Rick thing, and more than a work thing—It is a God thing in my mind and that makes me ÜberHappy! You are truly an incredible person and on top of everything else a great friend. The time we have together indeed does fly by at warp speed, but I enjoy each and every second of it! I am excited about the coming days as we continue down this path of happiness!

I love you,

R^2

see page 263

Naturally, my parents, friends, family, and coworkers wondered aloud if we were going to get married. We had never discussed our future. It was almost just understood. But as we sat one day talking, I mentioned that it seemed really foolish for me to get an apartment in Aubrey and pay deposits and everything else if we were going to be married soon. He shared his thoughts that we'd get married over the Thanksgiving holiday, coming up in a few months. And I was ecstatic yet practical as always. I addressed the fact that I'd still have to get an apartment and have unnecessary expenses for only a few months. I suggested, as crazy as it seemed, maybe we could get married before the new school year started, so that Macy and I could move only once and in with him.

Having already decided that we would not live together before getting married, simply moving in with him before the wedding was not an option. Rick was the only man I'd ever connected with on every level—spiritually, intellectually, emotionally. We were equally yoked. I didn't look at another man after I met Rick. I was extremely attracted to him, and I knew we'd also connect physically, but we decided that that was not what our relationship would be based on. The rapid timeline may suggest that our bond was based on a hot, physical whirlwind romance, but as passionate as we were, we knew that we wanted to wait until our wedding night.

Rick countered my suggestion with another. "I'll go one better, Abby. What if we just make New York our honeymoon?" And nothing had ever sounded so good.

We'd made the decision to marry and set a wedding date—the only thing missing was a proposal! Rick soon fixed that in his own incredibly thoughtful way. In June, a month before our wedding, Rick and I spoke at a UIL coaches' seminar in Austin, the site of our fateful first encounter. Sitting down to dinner at Oasis, where we'd shared that legendary first dinner, we enjoyed an intimate meal after a long day. As the sun set, the waitress brought a FedEx envelope to the table (Rick's clever reference to the night we confessed to love one another), with a CX debate ballot inside—oddly similar to the scoring ballot I'd received after meeting him, the ballot that had first sparked my interest. Removing it from the envelope, I read the ballot filled with Rick's words, listing all the reasons why he loved me and

① Wow! For eight weeks now that simple three letter word has been bouncing around my head & it so completely summarizes everything I have been thinking. Wow! You truly are an answer to my prayers Abby. It, of course, was through work & debate that we ever met in the first place. Even though neither of us claim to enjoy anything about cx debate, we will forever be indebted to the event & to your 2003 district meet!

CROSS-EXAMINATION DEBATE BALLOT

University Interscholastic League

Conference: **AA**   Date: **June 28, 2003**   Judge: **God**   Room: **anywhere**   Round: **anytime**

⑥ Affirmative Team # **all positives!**   Negative Team # **no negatives**

Circle the number on each category below representing your evaluation of each speaker. Rank each debater from 1 to 4 in order of excellence (1 for best, 2 for next best, 3 and 4). Delivery that interferes with effective communication should be penalized.

| 2 points—Below Average | | 3 points—Average | | 4 points—Good | | 5 points—Superior |

1st Affirmative Speaker	2nd Affirmative Speaker	*Voting Criteria*	1st Negative Speaker	2nd Negative Speaker
Name	Name		Name	Name
2 3 4 5	2 3 4 5	• Organization •	2 3 4 5	2 3 4 5
2 3 4 5	2 3 4 5	Evidence	2 3 4 5	2 3 4 5
2 3 4 5	2 3 4 5	Analysis	2 3 4 5	2 3 4 5
2 3 4 5	2 3 4 5	Refutation	2 3 4 5	2 3 4 5
2 3 4 5	2 3 4 5	Oral Style	2 3 4 5	2 3 4 5
2 3 4 5	2 3 4 5	• Speed of Delivery •	2 3 4 5	2 3 4 5
Total Points	Total Points		Total Points	Total Points
Speaker Rank	Speaker Rank		Speaker Rank	Speaker Rank

Write comments for each speaker below.

AFFIRMATIVE TEAM	NEGATIVE TEAM
② 1st Affirmative All of this 1st started with a quick glance & a nod at Lindale in February where we spent an entire weekend with our soulmate & NEVER knew it back then. Indeed God does work in mysterious ways & He must have had a plan for us VERY early on!	1st Negative ④ Austin, Texas has always been one of my favorite cities in the world to visit... & for even better reason now! I spent the entire 2002-2003 school year looking forward to UIL State Meet in May. Little did I realize just what a great & indeed life-changing weekend it would be.
③ 2nd Affirmative The very fact that I was asked (made!) to stay for that last cx round at your district meet could have been a real negative. As you can imagine, I was NOT a happy camper about being there. BUT luckily I did take the time to write a good ballot & fortunately you guys read it! My imaginary friend & I worked hard on said ballot that evening.	2nd Negative ⑤ Even while I was charging 25 feet in front of you at the Oasis, I was living a dream. Yup, Abby Soon-To-Be Riba, are everything I could ever hope for in a best friend, soulmate, wife, co-worker, & life-long companion. - See #6 on far left

The significant clash(es) / issue(s) used as the basis for my decision were:

⑦ After weeks of consideration ¨ & analyzing the situation, there is a single thought that continually resonates through my mind, body, & soul. My invisible friend & I have never met anyone as brilliant AND beautiful AND passionate about life AND fun AND understanding AND patient AND giving AND confident AND well-spoken AND thoughtful AND energetic AND ...
So... I was wondering - would you & Macy please marry me?... July 19... Under your parents Glad Oak?

In my judgment, the _____ (Affirmative or Negative) team won the debate.

_____
Signature of Judge

Manganos to public performances to your folks' house w/ Macy to the Leders' & Julie's porches to dinner w/ Raymond & the Menaces to Lindale to cx ballots to McDonald's play areas to Sweetwater to late-night phone discussions to Mavs-Spurs Game 6 to sitting around watching movies with Macy to sitting in Mr. C's office to puking w/ my mom to giggling over pictures of each other from the "UGLY YEARS" to re-telling our story to countless friends to morning e-mails & diet or vanilla cokes & now

[left margin, top] These past eight weeks we have been living & experiencing the "greatest love story of ALL time!" From the Oasis to

[right margin] 14 Ritz weeks, we are indeed the luckiest people on Earth. You and now for the next several decades are going to be as amazing as these past weeks, our love has been in it together. If in the next several decades are going to be as amazing as these past weeks, our love has been in it together. If in the decision to the decision we have been in it together... back to Austin this weekend...

—Rick's proposal to Abby

wanted to marry Macy and me, ending with, "So...I was wondering—would you and Macy please marry me?...July 19...under your parents' Glad Oak?" My reaction, after immediately saying "Yes," was to wonder how I could ever adequately tell or show him how perfect he was. He brought such peace, contentment, and blissful happiness to my life, and I marveled at his goodness. What did I do to deserve this man? Why was I so blessed to have someone who made me feel like the most wonderful, smart, funny, beautiful, desired woman in the world? Rick made me feel like the best version of myself. He made me see myself through his eyes. I was loved by the best man in the world.

Rick and I were far more concerned with our marriage than with our wedding, but my parents created the most beautiful setting imaginable. I had expressed my desire for it to be small, as it was a second marriage for both of us. We decided that it was not going to be a big deal and we'd marry under the Glad Oak in my parents' backyard. Over a hundred guests, a violinist, and an abundance of flowers later, it was our wedding day. I had planned to wear a modest pantsuit with a pink jacket, but it was overwhelmingly hot that day, and I opted for a black floral dress already hanging in my closet. We had a very brief ceremony, served fajitas, and wore simple matching wedding bands engraved with TEAM RIKE. And a team is what we were, for when Rick had placed a ring on my finger as a symbol of our commitment, he also placed a ring on Macy's.

So began our journey together in the greatest partnership that ever was.

Abby,

This card is so simple and so understated, yet so perfect. One of my favorite posters is the Jesus Footprints story, and this reminded me of it a bit. When I look at the wandering footprints of my life, I have no clue how I was fortunate enough to come face to face with you in Austin, TX, six weeks ago. And now, we are going to walk side by side for many weeks, months, and YEARS to come. How exciting is that? I am so glad we met indeed. I am also thrilled, blessed, fortunate, and thankful that we met. You truly are the love of my life. Everyone I have known to this point in my life pales in comparison to you, Abby Davis... You are leaving Canton, selling your house, looking at new houses, accepting a new job, and GETTING MARRIED! Wow! And it all seems so incredibly natural. I am so looking forward to this entire weekend, the rest of this summer, and indeed our lives together! I love you very much, Abby!

R^2

—Rick Rike, from a card depicting two footprints
in the sand, see page 263

CHAPTER 4

Growing Pains

In a successful marriage, there is no such thing as one's way. There is only the way of both, only the bumpy, dusty, difficult, but always mutual path.

—Phyllis McGinley

M uch like our dating life, the initial months of our marriage warranted rapid changes. I was taking a new position at Aubrey High School, getting to know new students in a brand-new place. Rick was opening his home to Macy and me, having left our home in Mabank to settle in Aubrey. The decision to move felt like the right one, and we were excited about building our family there. Rick and I had already engaged in discussions about the amazing team the two of us made and how we couldn't wait to bring "Team Rike" to the students in Aubrey's UIL program. We immediately set the goal to win the overall UIL state speech championship together. Still, our anticipation and excitement didn't take away from the fact that all three of our lives were about to undergo a major upheaval.

Rick was a man of tradition, a very stable person who did not adjust well to change. Once he got comfortable somewhere, he stayed. Rick was not one to move around or to take a risk. He'd sustained multiple high school friendships into college, student-taught at Aubrey High, and then built a career as a teacher there for the past seven years. In retrospect, Rick's traditional nature made our whirlwind courtship that much more unbelievable, especially since he wasn't the only one who made a point never to act impulsively. Like Rick, I rarely acted hastily in important decisions, but rather thought things through before committing. But I'd never met or even imagined a man as wonderful as Rick—joining my life with his was a privilege.

Dear Rick,

WOW! I can't believe it is actually happening . . . married . . . that is us. You are the man I've prayed for since I was eight years old. You are notorious for all your "stories," so I guess that explains why I'm getting to experience the greatest love story of all time! What a story it makes! More importantly, what a great life it makes!

You amaze me every day. It's hard to believe that I am able to love you more now than I did six weeks ago and to firmly know I will love you even more a year from now . . . ten years from now . . . fifty years from now . . .

I know we've talked about it before, but I truly would go through every part of my life and not change a thing so that I could be at this point in my life with you. I didn't know it, but you were the thing missing in my life. You are my split-apart,

and I thank God every day for you. It's hard to remember
life before you because I feel like I have known you forever . . .
luckily I get to spend forever with you.

Thank you for being the man you are . . . honorable and
sensitive and kind and passionate and creative and humble
and everything *I could want in a mate* and more. *My cup*
runneth over! I love and honor and adore you, and I promise
I will live my life so that one day you can say, "I've had a
great life!"

Abby Rike
see page 264

I realized soon after Macy was born that every decision
I made had to be in her best interest. She had not asked to
be born into a single-parent home. The life the two of us
led before meeting Rick was a result of my choices, and I
decided early on that I was not going to continue to make
mistakes. I happily placed Macy as my number one priority,
above all other things in my life, and I protected her at all
costs. I would never have uprooted her from Mabank had
I not known without a shadow of a doubt that Rick was
going to bring nothing but joy, stability, and love into our
lives. I always put Macy first, and Rick loved that about me.
He was never jealous of my love for her, and he respected
that I made all decisions with Macy in mind. Marrying
Rick and moving to Aubrey was a choice that I made without reservation, knowing that Macy's life would be that
much happier with Rick in it.

Before coming into our lives, Rick lived as a true

bachelor. Without a family demanding his time and attention, Rick had wholeheartedly devoted himself to work and friends. Suddenly, his new wife and her toddler were moving in to his life and his house. And nothing said "bachelor" as much as Rick's one-bedroom, one-bathroom duplex—"cramped" was a huge understatement. I affectionately referred to his place as the "Shanty." There we were, newlyweds, sharing our bedroom with Macy, who slept on an inflated mattress next to our bed, trying to adjust to the intricacies of living together in an environment where we and our belongings were literally on top of each other. Our separate lives had come together as one in a beautiful but chaotic fashion.

Mild stresses at home were far exceeded by the strain I began to feel in my new position at Aubrey High. I taught the theater classes as I had at Canton High, along with a video productions class of which I knew almost nothing. Rick began teaching a history class that year and continued in his job as the coordinator of Aubrey's UIL program. I joined him as a coach in the program to pursue the goal we'd set to win an overall state speech championship. I focused on the prose and poetry categories, working with students' delivery, introductions, and anything else that went into the speaking element of competition. Rick handled the entire program as UIL coordinator. He procured materials, scheduled buses, oversaw budgets, and trained other coaches, all while coaching various categories himself: spelling, journalism, current issues, and history. His work ethic was inspiring and unparalleled.

Rick was an enormously effective teacher; his ability to communicate not only his passion for the subject matter but his love for each student endeared him to every kid who crossed his path. The respect he showed his students was mirrored back to him, and Rick very rarely dealt with discipline problems—a fortunate situation, since he was not a disciplinarian by nature. Although I shared Rick's teaching philosophy, I was much more comfortable than he was with taking on an authoritative role when necessary. We worked as perfect complements to each other's strengths. Rick researched topics and provided the background information students needed to understand their subject matter, while I ensured that the speeches were aesthetically pleasing and the delivery was unforgettable. He gave them the substance, and I molded the finished product. Our work as a team created incredible depth of talent in our program.

Rick and I took pride in the service we provided for our students, and our work was validated by Dr. James Monaco, the superintendent we affectionately called "Doc" (although Rick always had far too much respect for him to call him anything but Dr. Monaco to his face). One of Rick's biggest fans, Dr. Monaco always valued Rick's passion and skill as a teacher. He loved Rick like a son and delighted in seeing him develop into a family man. Dr. Monaco loved my teaching style and thought our different approaches created the perfect balance. He supported our relationship so completely because he was able to see Rick becoming the best version of himself—growing into the man he always knew he would be.

Although we worked closely during UIL practices, we rarely saw each other during the school day other than sharing lunch together in one of our classrooms. Still, it was an adjustment for Rick's coworkers and friends who didn't take well to his lifestyle changes. Rick was suddenly not as available to them as he'd been before. He was married and had a child now, so naturally some elements of his bachelorhood didn't remain. As a single man, he'd often go to dinner with friends on a weeknight. He could easily hold UIL practice until seven or eight o'clock in the evening and attend countless UIL tournaments. But now, Rick had a family to consider, and his time was regularly filled by the demands of a child and a domestic life. Those who'd grown accustomed to the way Rick used to be soon began to blame me for his detachment, and the work environment at Aubrey High became very difficult. In my naïveté, I thought, *They love Rick. I love Rick. He loves me, so they'll love me, too.* But that did not happen. I felt very ostracized and became quite distant due to hurt feelings and perceived unfair judgment. I was constantly on guard and had never felt so unwelcome and lonely at work; therefore, very few people there got to know me on a personal level. I was overwhelmed, adjusting to a different place and job, caring for Macy without the family support I'd relied on in Canton, while trying to nurture a new marriage. Rick, eager to avoid confrontation when possible, chose to deal with the conflict by ignoring it, allowing unfounded negativity to continuously invade my workspace. It was an uncomfortable situation—one I wouldn't have gotten through so successfully without the two women who were my saving grace at Aubrey High: Jodee Heimdal and Pam McDonald.

Jodee embraced me and loved me from the moment I settled in Aubrey. She also taught the video productions class and helped me enormously with that course. Her kindness and beauty was emulated in her three precious girls—Lexi, Jessi, and Kalsi—who were perfect playmates for Macy. They doted on her and took her in as a fourth sister. I particularly bonded with Jodee's middle child, Jessi, who was absolutely delightful. She was in grade school at the time—not a stage of childhood I'm typically drawn to—but Jessi was special. Engaged by her extraordinary, bubbly personality, I formed a connection with her immediately and loved Jessi immensely. Having Jodee and her girls in my life was a blessing that got me through many hard days in Aubrey.

Pam McDonald knew Rick well and loved him, and she received me with equal love and acceptance. I was lucky enough to have an off period with her every other day. We would take a ride together, and she'd let me vent. I honestly don't know if my marriage would have been as solid as it was if I had not known Pam McDonald that year. She saw what was going on with other teachers on the staff who hadn't accepted Rick's new life as a married man. With Pam, I didn't have to defend myself or explain anything. Her familiarity with Rick allowed me to share any frustrations I had over the tiny space where we lived, the isolation I felt at work, or anything weighing on my mind. She understood that neither Rick nor I was perfect, but that we loved each other and were good for each other. She gave us a fair chance, and because of her, I didn't have to keep everything bottled up.

Despite anxiety in the workplace, Rick and I did not take those issues home with us. We did not allow it to affect our relationship and focused on fostering a marriage based on mutual respect and love. Rick and I never wasted energy on needless fights over household chores or daily duties. If something needed to be done around the house, we did it and in no way felt like we had to institute a division of domestic roles. Even in the most mundane tasks, we always worked so solidly as a team, and our household ran without unnecessary tension.

We stayed connected by falling back on what had drawn us to each other in the first place. The conversations we'd had while dating continued into our marriage, and we would talk incessantly before bed each night. We discussed our day and never let any negative feelings build. I realized that it was not in Rick's nature to discuss his feelings; he typically put his emotions aside rather than deal with them outright. But when it came to our relationship, his willingness to involve me in his thoughts and feelings created a safe place for both of us to be ourselves. If something bothered him or me, we talked about it without being confrontational. If I was impatient or snappish, Rick would simply bring that to my attention so I could change my tone. I was always very clear about what I needed from him instead of playing games and expecting him to figure out what was bothering me. Neither of us had any problems admitting our faults, so we were able to apologize when necessary and move on. Communication was paramount in our marriage, and with that as our foundation, we formed an impermeable bond.

Rick's transformation from bachelor to family man took place before my eyes, as I witnessed his and Macy's budding relationship. Macy and I were a package deal. Loving me meant loving Macy, and Rick knew what he was signing up for before he ever pursued dating me. I later learned that long before meeting me Rick had made it clear to his friends that he didn't want to have children. Fatherhood was not a role he planned to take on. All the same, our paths had crossed that weekend in Austin and his life took a turn he wasn't expecting. Never once did Rick say a word to me about not wanting children. Had that conversation taken place after we started dating, I would have ended things and sent him on his way. I would have been sad and shed tears about it, but I would have swiftly ended a relationship with anyone who did not welcome and love my Macy. That was never a concern with Rick; it was clear from his interactions with her that his intentions were to love us both. He was never anything but patient and kind and understanding.

Our family dynamic was different from what might occur in a "natural" family where two people meet, marry, and have children together. As a single parent remarrying, I brought an existing parent-child relationship into a new marriage. Since day one of Macy's life, I'd built a working family system of respect, support, discipline, and joy based on limitless, unconditional love. It was a huge step for me to invite someone else to be a part of my most treasured blessing: my life with Macy. Still, I was so certain that Rick was the one I'd prayed for countless times, the one who'd fill the void in our family life.

As I mentioned previously, per the conditions of the divorce, my ex-husband was not allowed unsupervised visits with Macy until she turned three years old. He chose to make approximately three supervised visits in those three years, so Macy had very little knowledge of life with a dad. Macy did have the benefit of a loving relationship with her grandmother, Monica, and her great-grandparents. They adored Macy, were nothing but supportive of me as a parent, and made every effort to come to birthday parties and visit as much as possible. Macy enjoyed those times, and it was important to me to cultivate that bond for her sake. With Macy's well-being always in mind, I decided early on that I would never vindictively turn Macy against my ex-husband. Looking back, I can unreservedly say that I never said anything negative about him to Macy. By no means did I ever debase him or discuss the situation in any way in Macy's presence, because that would have brought nothing positive to her life. Little girls need to hear and know that their dads are wonderful and that their dads love them, whether it's true or not. So I did everything I possibly could to tell Macy that her dad adored her and just happened to live in a different town. I feared one day her opinion might change, but their relationship would not be negatively shaped by me.

I was just as steadfast in my decision to allow Macy and Rick to develop their own connection at a natural rate. I never pushed a relationship between the two of them, because forced relationships are just that. Forced. I wanted their bond to be genuine and comfortable. Luckily, Rick and I shared a common vision for our domestic life together. He certainly did not expect to come into the stepparent role as an authority over Macy, nor did I want that from him. Rick was more than happy to let me handle discipline issues with Macy; he never overstepped his boundaries or made me feel uneasy. In turn, I was quite comfortable with those duties and had no problem being the bad guy. It didn't bother me if Macy threw a fit or was mad at me for the moment.

Exceptionally gifted, Macy understood things on a level that other children her age weren't able to comprehend. She had a capacity for language and an understanding of the subtleties in life that were beyond her years. I could discuss things with her from a very young age. I'd often explain, "Parents who don't love their children give them everything they want. Parents who love their children tell them 'No' and then put up with these little fits. I love you enough to put up with them, and I know you're going to be a better person for it. Just know that I do this because I adore you, but I'm not going to let you be a monster. So throw a fit, do what you need to do, but this is how it is." And for the most part, she got it and had a considerable respect for my authority.

Still, Macy did not make an automatic transition from

having my undivided attention to now having to share me with Rick. Accustomed to having me all to herself, Macy was territorial toward this man who had come into our lives so quickly. She was two and a half at the time and approached everything new with the utmost vigor and passion; in those early months with Rick as a new family, she channeled that into being as difficult as possible. She always referred to him as "Rick Rike," which we thought was too precious. Macy certainly did not make things easy for Rick, but he could not have been more consistent, even-keeled, or considerate. For a man who had once said he had no desire for children, Rick so naturally fell into the fatherly role, it was uncanny. He loved Macy from the beginning, as an extension of his love for me; but Macy's spirit and love of life were infectious, and Rick was not immune. He soon fell in love with her all on his own, and they built a relationship sustained by bonds of love and trust. He and Macy played together with such ease, Rick sitting on the floor playing with Barbies—in such a masculine, endearing way. He was always better at pretending and joining in the fantasy games she created than I had ever been. Their interactions were beautiful to watch and unlike anything I'd ever witnessed. As our marriage continued, I encouraged him to be a bit more firm with Macy if the situation warranted, and eventually he became comfortable with placing her in a time-out and addressing certain issues. Macy gained a natural respect for his authority, and as he showed her the wealth of love and security he had to share, Macy grew to see him as that constant in her life—that father figure she'd not known up to this point.

Macy settled quickly into our new life in Aubrey and began attending a day care at the elementary school. Rick and I picked her up each day after school, and we'd spend the afternoons together at home or take Macy along to UIL practices at Aubrey High. One particular day in late September, just a couple of months shy of three years old, Macy came out of day care with an inquisitive expression. Perhaps she had noticed other children leaving with their dads, for after she climbed into the car and we left, she asked, "Where's my daddy?" Her question sent faint pangs of guilt through my body as I nonchalantly answered, "Well, baby, your daddy lives in Houston. Every family is different, and some daddies just live in other places." She sat there quietly for a minute, her brilliant mind absorbing and analyzing that information. Rick unpretentiously drove along as her unexpected response came from the backseat. "Rick Rike, will you be my daddy?"

Tears immediately stung my eyes. I was stunned and overwhelmed by emotion all at the same time. We had never referred to Rick as "Daddy." She was so young, and I hadn't anticipated a question like that until years down the road. Rick was instantly ready with his answer. "Oh, of course, baby! I love you, and I would love to be your daddy." She continued, "Can I call you Daddy?" Rick, always with Macy's interests in mind, stressed to her, "You can call me Daddy; you can call me Rick Rike. You call me whatever you want to call me." And we drove on as though that momentous exchange between the two of them was a normal part of our day.

It took Macy about two or three weeks before she

exclusively called Rick "Daddy." In that time I made a point to reiterate to her that it was her choice. She alternated between "Rick Rike" and "Daddy," testing it out, seeing how it felt, but a few weeks before her third birthday, she made her decision and chose Rick as her dad, a man who could not have loved her any more had she been his own child—a marvel too great to have occurred without God's divine arrangement.

Dearest Rick,

It's hard to believe we've been married a month! It's even harder to believe how much my life has changed since I met you such a short time ago. You have brought such joy to my life! Thank you!

As I reflect back over the journey that brought me to this place, I realize I have never loved a man until you. You are everything a husband should be . . . kind, patient, giving, willing to talk things through, romantic, affectionate, and a true leader. Thank you!

You "wow" me on a daily basis. My Macy has now become our Macy. I don't know if I ever thought I could share her rearing with anyone, but you make it so easy. You touch my heart every time you read to her or give her a bath or tell her bedtime stories. You are such an incredible dad! You love her even when she's being somewhat unloveable. That takes a very strong man. Thank you!

If this month is indicative of the next fifty years, then I will have lived a blessed life. It is my prayer that I will be the kind of wife you need and deserve for the next fifty years. Our

*foundation is strong and our future is so bright! Together we
can face anything.*

*Thank you for making me a part of the greatest love story
of all time. I can't promise that it will always be easy facing
the challenges of life, but I can promise that I will love, honor,
respect, adore, and cherish you til death do us part!*

I do so love you, Rick!

Abby

see page 265

With Macy's third birthday quickly approaching, we
were faced with the daunting reality that unsupervised visitation with my ex-husband was about to begin. I'd been
successful at ensuring that any interaction between him and
Macy had to be supervised, but that stipulation no longer
applied as soon as Macy turned three. A huge consolation
was that my ex-mother-in-law, Monica, and I had a great
relationship. I knew Macy was comfortable with her, and I
found great solace in knowing that in my absence Monica
would ensure Macy's happiness and safety.

With the start of the new year in January, Rick and I
continued to build Team Rike at Aubrey High, enjoying
great success with the students as they improved and grew
to be extremely competitive. With a state championship in
speaking as our goal, Rick and I decided to eliminate the
cross-examination, partner debate category, from our program. CX debate was so time-consuming and required such
an intense amount of work; we needed that time to become
as competitive as possible in Lincoln-Douglas debate. This

move came with a risk, since we'd receive zero points in the CX category at the state meet, but we knew we would have a better chance of achieving our goal by focusing all our energy on the remaining events. Everyone was working tirelessly to make our dream of a championship a reality, but after almost six months in Aubrey, professional success had taken a backseat to our family life.

We were regularly driving to Mabank every other weekend, staying in my old house, which had remained on the market since Macy and I moved to Aubrey. We were so comfortable there, and the longer the house remained unsold, the harder it was to keep finding reasons to stay in Aubrey. In February at my dear friend Kelli's wedding, I ran into her uncle—none other than Max Callahan, my former principal at Canton High. Max informed me there was going to be an opening in my old job, and I immediately told him that I wanted it. Even with no job prospects in Canton for Rick, we both agreed that a move back into my old house in Mabank was the best decision for our family.

Meanwhile, Macy had gone to see my ex-husband once in late November and again in December. Each time I would take her to Mabank and meet him or take her all the way to Houston.

Soon it was spring, and Rick and I had a full plate. We were hosting a tournament and working nonstop. My ex-husband called, wanting me to bring Macy to Mabank to meet him. I told him he'd have to come get her because we were hosting a tournament that weekend and driving was not possible. Driving to Aubrey instead of Mabank added a few hours to his drive, and he did not react well to the idea. I kept my tone even and calm, but he eventually hung up on me, only to call back ten minutes later. I fully anticipated another painful exchange. After my guarded "Hello," he countered with "Does Rick want to adopt Macy?" That was the last thing I ever expected to hear. Rick and I had never discussed it; I hadn't thought it was even an option. Before the divorce was finalized, I had suggested a termination of rights, but my ex-husband had refused. I responded to his question. "I'm sure that could be arranged." He instructed me, "You have a week to draw up the papers, and you're paying for all of it."

Hanging up the phone, I immediately had to do a gut check. *I'm about to give Rick legal rights to my child.* Instant peace. There were no feelings of anxiety, worry, or uncertainty. I was perfectly at peace with it, and that was a huge step for me. I never thought I'd ever give anyone rights to Macy. But Rick wanted nothing more than to be her daddy. When I told him what my ex-husband had suggested, Rick was shocked for an instant, then elated. With tears in his eyes, he expressed his relief that Macy would not have to travel back and forth on mandatory weekends and split every other holiday. We were both beyond grateful that we would all have the same last name. It was an amazing transition for a man to go from believing that he never wanted children to now loving Macy more than some biological fathers love their children. He could have passed a lie detector test saying that she was his. He'd fallen in love with her innocence, her brilliance, her humor. He was the most consistent, even-keeled, steady father, and he could not have loved Macy any more than he did. She was his; we just had to make it legal. Adoptions take a long time, but I was miraculously able to find an attorney who could take our case and do it in Canton. Once the papers for termination of rights were drawn up and signed, the weight of the world was off my shoulders.

I stayed in frequent contact with Max, and soon enough, he let us know there would be an opening for a speech teacher at Canton High if Rick was interested. Because of the decision to make the move back to Mabank, we were beyond grateful to both have positions at Canton for the next school year. Then suddenly, in an unexpected turn of events, the UIL coordinator at Canton resigned—opening the exact position Rick currently held at Aubrey. In addition, Rick and I would be team-teaching a debate class. It was confirmation that this move was meant to be, and we were so excited about what life held for us.

Back in Aubrey, Rick and I had an amazing professional year with UIL. We loved the students and took thirteen of fifteen speech kids to the regional tournament. We won the regional meet and were alternate to state for our play. As the state tournament approached, Rick and I were elated with our students' success and felt confident about our chances to accomplish the goal we'd set ten months earlier.

My Dearest Rick,
So I'm hoping this will look original, this whole writing in a folder thing, rather than I've had no time to get you the

"perfect" card. ☺ But then again, that is what makes us so special.

I'm almost overwhelmed tonight by how much I love you. You absolutely amaze me. You make me feel so loved and appreciated. There is no man on this earth that could ever compare to you. When I was at my lowest point several years ago, and I cried out to God to send me a Godly, manly-man who was sensitive and kind and good, I had no idea He would surpass my wildest fantasies with you. I love everything about you . . . from the way you love Macy to the way I feel safe in your arms . . . from the way you are the ultimate optimist to the way you can fall asleep faster than any human I've ever known . . . a sign of the clearest conscience! ☺ You are the perfect man for me.

This year has definitely been a challenge, and I am so sorry for all the times I've been selfish thinking it was harder for me. It is such a small price to pay to get to wake up in your arms each day. Please forgive that selfishness. I will be better.

This is your year to shine professionally. I want you to savor every second of your success because you deserve it! There will be no one more proud for you and of you when you get your first UIL state champion pins this year! I must admit a small (or maybe large) part of me is thrilled to get to share that with you.

I have a great feeling about this weekend. Don't underestimate for one second what an amazing coach you are. If anyone is the Pied Piper, it is you. You inspire everyone around you to be their personal best . . . that includes kids, adults, and luckily for me, me! Thank you for being the role model you are!

You are the man of my dreams and the greatest love of my life. I thank God every day for you. And as a very wise man

*once said . . . if these seven months are any indication of how
our lives will be, then we are the luckiest people on earth.*
I do so love and adore you, Wallace Richard Rike!
Abby
—*written inside of a manila folder, see page 266*

At the state tournament in May, we won the overall
state speech championship by a landslide—even without
points in CX debate. Rick got his first state champion pin
in persuasive speaking and was ecstatic. But even amid such
great accomplishments at Aubrey High, Rick and I never
doubted our impending move. Our careers were not defining us anymore. Personal growth and our home life were
more important than anything else.

We stayed in Aubrey until the end of that school year. Dr.
Monaco, in spite of the fact that Rick and I burdened him
with finding replacements for both of us, was supportive and
positive about our decision to move. He wanted what was best
for Rick, the man, so we left on the best terms with him.

Though our time in Aubrey was a challenge in many
aspects, I never doubted that choice. I always felt at peace
that God's hand had been in that decision. Rick needed
me there for that year until he got to a place where he was
ready to leave. And for Rick, who did not adjust well to
change, he needed that year to adjust to family life before
taking on a new work life. He was ready to leave his old life
behind—one he'd led for over seven years. But what mattered now was not what we used to have, because anything
we'd experienced in the past paled in comparison to the

present. All that we cared about was being together in a healthy environment for our family.

Abigail,

Where has the time gone dear wife of mine? Was it really ten months ago today we were under the Glad Oak? That day was very special and one I still think about every day of my life. The best decision I ever made was getting married to you and Macy. The last three hundred days have been the happiest of my life. The joy you bring on a daily basis surpasses anything I ever dreamt possible. I thank God every day that we have our time together. Time is something that is so easy to take for granted. The fact is we have no clue how long we have together. We might have sixty minutes, sixty days, or sixty months together. I hope we have sixty years ahead of us to watch Macy grow up, build our dream house together, win state championships, and grow closer and closer together. The fact is I cherish all of our days, our nights, and our conversations together. Never have I cared for anyone or anything like I care for our family. The comfort that comes from knowing we will spend eternity together is wonderful.

Of course there will be times in our lives when time flies or we get busy or we are less attentive, but my prayer is those times are fleeting. The fact is I truly believe we just endured the toughest four and a half months we will ever face together. Not only leaving here, but leaving so many obligations behind will pave the way to much easier times in future years. Never again will we have the challenges we had this year. Never again will we have people trying to undermine who we are and what we do. As I have said time and again, the fact we could survive this semester and this year speaks volumes to who we are and what we have. If we could bottle this up and sell it, we would have our millions we want! ☺ I am so anxious to get out of Tioga, to get out of Aubrey, and to get on with our lives. The future indeed seems so very bright. This summer will be great, next year at Canton will be wonderful—certainly not perfect as that isn't realistic—but wonderful. I look forward to working for and with YOUR people. I have all the confidence that will work out and we will have a great time together.

Another way I know just how much I love you is because of the fact I am not stressing about my work future. I love you so much that I really don't care if I am a Walmart greeter or a mechanic or a high school computer teacher. I simply want to spend time with you, love you, dote on you, kiss you, talk to you, share my life with you, and grow old with you. Everything else is trivial at this point. We are going to quickly put this year and our experience here to rest . . . Soon we will be able to enjoy normal life in Mabank and if life gets better than this, I am one LUCKY man! Thank you for the greatest ten months of marriage ever!

I love you!

R^2

see page 267

Dear Rick,

Every day you amaze me with what a wonderful person you are! You are hands down the best father any little girl could dream of having! You are so consistently patient and kind. You say you've learned about parenting from me, but I've learned so much from you.

In addition to being an amazing father, you are a remarkable husband as well. You make me feel so loved and adored and cherished and respected. I never in my wildest dreams imagined married life could be this blissful. You are the easiest person to love. I fall more in love with you with each passing day. Not only are you extraordinarily handsome, you are so witty and intelligent and so fun to be around.

I know it's hard to experience so much change. I have to believe that God has a perfect plan for us, and I truly believe that we are supposed to be in Canton. Everyone is going to absolutely love you. The kids are going to be so happy to have you around to work with them and help them be their personal best! We make a great team . . . as husband and wife, as mother and father, and as educators. My life is complete with you.

Thank you for being my soul mate, best friend, number one supporter, father of our child, and the greatest husband anyone could ever ask for!

I do so love and adore you!

Abby
see page 268

CHAPTER 5

Team Rike

Family faces are magic mirrors. Looking at people who
belong to us, we see the past, present, and future.
    —*Gail Lumet Buckley,* The Hornes: An American Family

L
ife could not have been better. Rick, Macy, and I had
benefited from the most wonderful turn of events.
We were back in the home Macy and I had always
known, and Rick and I felt so blessed to have our positions
at Canton High. I slipped right back into the work I'd been
doing before leaving for Aubrey and even got to team-teach
the debate class with Rick. In addition to his duties as UIL
coordinator, Rick also taught the speech classes. Being a
man of tradition, he was scared to death to be at a new
school in a new job. He had always been the best teacher at
Aubrey, beloved by the students and the head of an amazing program. He took that work ethic and focused it on the
program at Canton, wanting to do his best work to date.
In accepting the job as UIL coordinator, Rick replaced a
teacher whose main focus had been literary criticism. The

rest of the program was quite disjointed, leaving Rick with the perfect opportunity to reshape the way things would be done. He was the perfect man for the job. As a teacher, Rick was innately patient, kind, and encouraging. He had such a passion for kids and wanted so badly for them to experience the feeling of success and carry that on with them into adulthood. Rick cared immensely and taught from a place of love that attracted students in search of a place to fit in. I learned so much from Rick about UIL. We recruited teachers together and formed a wonderfully cohesive group.

In small towns in Texas, the focus is predominately on sports, rather than academics. Every kid wants to belong to something, to have a "home"; our program provided students with opportunities to find their place. Students did not have to be "gifted" to be a part of Team Rike. Students didn't have to be star speakers, or great competitors; we just loved them and brought them into the fold. We welcomed athletes, band members, cheerleaders, and students involved in nothing. From math, to spelling, to current issues, to the play, there was something for everyone, and that's what made it such a comfortable place to be. The team was something for kids to buy into, to be a part of, to care about—something bigger than themselves. Rick and I built a true family in our work with the kids; it surpassed the scope of a typical extracurricular activity.

Rick and I were once again the perfect complement to each other. Where I was weak (making lists, getting buses, sending out parent notes, lesson planning, paperwork), Rick was perfect. He handled it and never let it show as a stress. Where he was weak (creativity, introductions, facial expressions, delivery), I took over. There was never competition between the two of us; we were so united. That's hard to find in a work partner. We had the same exact teaching philosophy, so we never had to worry, *Is he/she telling them something different from what I'd tell them?* I had such a deep respect for him that I never had to question, *Does he know what he's doing? Is he teaching something wrong?* I couldn't have shared my program, and he couldn't have shared his program, with someone that required cleaning up after. If he was working with a group, they were handled, so I then had time to concentrate on a different group. My time wasn't split. The kids got so much more out of it. If Rick thought I would better serve a question, he'd send them to me. And I would do the same. We both knew what we wanted done, and our vision was the same.

We truly loved each and every student in our program, but I cannot deny special bonds with certain kids. I had been extremely close with the kids in my interp group. Still, Jessica Cozart held an exclusive role. She was much more than a student to us; she was an adopted daughter. Rick and I both taught Jessica in our regular classes and had independently decided that she was amazing. When her name surfaced in conversation one day, we were both ecstatic to hear that the other had also fallen in love with Jessica's unique intelligence and depth. As a freshman, Jessica went to state in spelling and went on to compete in several academic events as a sophomore. Beyond her accomplishments in UIL, Rick, Macy, and I truly enjoyed Jessica's company. When practices ran late, we'd take Jessica home or invite her along for a meal at Two Senoritas, our favorite restaurant. She, as well as another student, Shae Akin, was a perfect, doting companion for Macy during practices and off campus. The Cozarts were the only people outside of my family I trusted to keep Macy overnight.

As married coworkers, we were unique role models for the students. Every day they saw what a solid marriage looked like—one of love and respect, but always with complete professionalism. On our free time, we held hands; we were very affectionate. We held hands in the car, everywhere we went. We were a little starry-eyed for one another. But not at work! Still, we were able to use our bond to form a great family. Rick's influence especially was quite powerful, when most students' teachers are women. They're used to a nurturing woman. But seeing such a caring man, a perfect father figure, was tremendously impactful to so many of the students.

We talked about school a lot at home, and we strategized. Rick spent countless hours with the other academic events, figuring out how we could win, where we could win, looking at scores across the state to see what we needed. We carried the excitement of work home, not the burdens. Our relationship was so fluid because I cared about what he cared about and vice versa. We could talk easily without having to give the background of every story. Nothing in our lives was separate; we shared it all.

Before Rick, I would have looked at a couple like us and wondered why they spent so much time together. I would have thought something must be wrong there. That's not healthy; you can't just have your spouse. But that's not true. I know because I lived it. It's obviously different if one person is guilting the other into spending that much time together or manipulating the relationship in some way. But Rick and Macy and I wanted nothing else but to be together. We simply liked each other more than we liked anyone else! Married couples should want to spend time together. Your spouse should be your best friend, the person you talk to. Your girlfriends should not know more about you than your spouse. After working and serving in the school with our students, there was so little free time, and we weren't sharing it. We were going to spend it together. We went to Macy's gymnastics classes together, to the grocery store, to my parents' house. And it never felt like a chore; I did exactly what I wanted to do. I had no problems telling people no. I didn't do things because I was supposed to. I wanted to watch Macy do gym; I wanted to go to the bookstore with Rick. Unapologetically, I was selfish with our family time. When there is limited time, you have to prioritize, and I was not giving to someone else, when I'd rather be giving to my family.

As Rick and I developed Team Rike at school, Macy was an integral part of our activities. We were able to find a day care that was right by Canton High, called Lil One's Academy. She was almost four at that time and at an age when she needed to be around other kids in a more structured environment. The day care was one mile from our school, so we were able to include her in after-school practices and in the lives of our students. Never without a play-mate, Macy always had someone's undivided attention. Rick and I enjoyed every moment spent with her; we were the parents who wanted nothing more than to watch her do gymnastics, draw, pretend, or just have fun in her incredibly precocious way. She continued to amaze Rick and me with how extraordinary she truly was.

Little Macy,

What a big day Monday is going to be! Your FIRST day of gymnastics class. I hope you know how incredibly proud your mother and I are of you. You are the most intelligent, sweetest, loving, and most beautiful child in the world. You are such a joy to have in my life. You are everything every daddy could ever need or want in a daughter. You have accepted me with open arms over the past year, and I will forever be indebted to you for that. Thank you so much for accepting me into your family. Now the Rike family is growing and maturing together. I am so excited about not only your gym class, but other things going on in our lives. We are also going to be taking one step closer to other things after today. There will be a day later in your life when you are an all star gymnast that everyone is reading about in the newspaper . . . they will say, "Wow—that Macy Marie Rike is really something. She is a great Texan, a great American, and a great daughter. Her parents sure must be proud of her." And you know what— they will be right. The thing is there is no doubt about the fact you are a winner. Whether you choose gym or sports or academics or politics or band or whatever—you are going to be successful. And . . . no matter what, we will always be proud of you. You just have to remember to be determined, be patient, be kind, and above all else . . . NEVER give up. You are an amazing little girl, and we are the luckiest parents in the world because we get to watch you grow up every day!

I love you with all my heart,

R^2

Daddy

—written June 6, 2004, see page 269

In October, the adoption process was finally coming to a close. Rick had to be fingerprinted; Macy got a new birth certificate and social security card. The day we appeared in court to finalize the adoption Rick had to give a statement, and within about five minutes we had certified copies declaring her Macy Marie Rike. I kept Macy as informed as she needed to be in an age-appropriate way. I never mentioned my ex-husband's decision to terminate his rights, and she never asked. It was just as natural a transition as everything had been since Rick had entered our lives.

CHAPTER 6

Baby Huey

Every child born into the world is a new thought of God, an ever-fresh and radiant possibility.

—*Kate Douglas Wiggin*

Coming into our second year at Canton High, Rick and I were beyond content with our marriage and our family. We'd briefly discussed extending our family with another child, but it was not a pressing concern. We felt that our life was about as perfect as it got. Macy was wonderful; we were enjoying our jobs at Canton; we savored every activity together. Life was great.

At the state tournament with our students in May 2005, we heard news that spurred further conversation between Rick and me. We found out that Natalie, a senior girl in our program, had been feeling very tired and was admitted to the hospital. She was then quickly diagnosed with leukemia, had an adverse reaction to treatment, and died two days after our return from the state tournament. It was absolutely devastating. Rick and I talked about her mother Susie who taught with us, and discussed, *What do you do if you lose your child when they're a senior in high school?* By that time, we'd be forty-five years old, and we only have one child. Not that you can ever replace a child. Susie had another daughter; not that she replaces Natalie in any capacity, but she still had those activities, that wedding, that life, those grandkids. And I thought, *If anything ever happened to Macy, I don't know what I would do.* We cried and talked about how family was our priority. We knew things would change at school if we had a new baby. The focus would shift. We wouldn't be able to do as much. But what was our real priority? I told Rick I wanted big Christmases, big Thanksgivings, and grandkids. Ultimately, it's about family. He felt the same way. So we decided we were going to try to have a baby! Not in a neurotic crazy way—we were just going to let it happen if it was meant to be.

The summer and fall went by, and nothing happened. When January came around, Rick noticed I was late before I did. We bought a test that morning, and I took it in the school bathroom—two lines after only about fifteen seconds! Rick came around after anxiously waiting, and with a grin, I said, "Houston, we've got a problem." I was scared, but then immediately overcome with joy and excitement. Rick was glowing, giddy with happiness, but not without worry. He was concerned about what kind of father he was going to be to a newborn baby, expressing his fear of such a tiny baby. I assured him he already was a phenomenal father and reminded him that every man and every woman feels that way.

Abigail Denise,

Wow! What a unique Valentine's Day this is. We are pregnant! ☺ *I never imagined I could be this happy over having a little Rikeling on the way. Wow! We are pregnant! Our love is truly a unique thing I know. We are so lucky to have the love that we have. Most people look forward to V-Day because it is one of the few days of the year where they feel loved. Lucky for me, I feel loved every day of the year. You do an incredible job of making sure I feel loved in so many ways. I love the way you scratch my back when I most need it. I love the way you look at me w/adoring eyes. I love the way you let me know you think I am a good husband. I love the way you let me be a true father to Macy. I love the way you go so far to show me you do care about my interests. Whether it is sports, politics, or whatever, I know you truly do care just because you know it is important at that moment to me. And . . . I love the way you are so excited about having our baby! I am so thrilled!* ☺

My resolution for the coming year is to be more and more thoughtful . . . You are the absolute perfect wife for me . . . and I am going to continue to strive to be the perfect husband to you. This new edition to our family is indeed going to change things—that is a given. I have no doubt at all that this is going to continue the greatest period of my life. For someone who was never going to have kids, I sure have done a 180°— Now maybe we should have four or five more . . . well—maybe not. ☺ *But I have every confidence that I am going to love raising our children together. You are the perfect mother to Macy. I am going to have to learn from you again about this whole infant parenting. I am so looking forward to it. You are truly an amazing wife, mother, best friend, parenting buddy, and Valentine. I have you a little present in the freezer.* ☺

Top Seven Things that are likely to change with the arrival of Reagan/Austin/Lauren/Elisabeth D.D. Rike:

7. *Walmart trips for pictures of TWO!*
6. *Macy starts to crave "alone time"*
5. *More manly shampoos appear in our shower*
4. *UIL slides down another notch in importance*
3. *Mack who? (at least for Fall 2006)* ☺
2. *My sleeping patterns.*
1. *My phobia of dirty diapers!*

One thing that will never change: my never-ending love for YOU!

I love you,
R^2
see pages 270 and 271

I was so happy that there was going to be a baby, but I was apprehensive of the actual pregnancy. I did not glow when I was pregnant with Macy five years prior. I knew I'd be swollen. I knew my nose was going to swell across my face. I knew I was going to be tired and sick. And I knew there was going to be a foreign object growing in my body at a rapid pace. I was willing to go through that because the end result was worth it. But I knew I was in for a long haul.

I was thirty-two and overweight—well over two hundred pounds. The pregnancy was hard on my body. My feet were swollen; I had blood pressure issues. I went for two days of the new school year in August 2006, then I went on bed rest. He eventually grew to over nine and a half pounds, leading Rick to refer to him affectionately as Baby Huey, after the oversized cartoon duck.

Despite the physical drudgery, my pregnancy was a time of great excitement and joy. Rick and I spent countless hours dreaming. We'd seen our first dream realized in baby Caleb, the completion of our family. Rick and I were quite excited about business ventures we'd recently undertaken. He was starting a business issuing study materials for current issues and had also looked into buying a company that provided spelling software for students. We'd crunched the numbers from these new projects and were so excited about the potential to supplement our income. We discussed me leaving teaching to stay home full time with Caleb and run the businesses. With more income we were then open to the possibility of building our dream home one day. Rick would sit and make these lists of upcoming years and what grades Macy and Caleb would be in and when we could afford to build our dream home. He had a spreadsheet! Mapped out. We had our five-year plan.

One hot summer day in particular we traveled to Dallas for one of our normal "dates." We were in our old '96 Toyota Camry with broken door handles on both sides, but the best air-conditioning you have ever experienced. We drove through North Dallas, in these affluent areas in our dilapidated Camry, dreaming about what our home might look like one day. He teased me when I ogled the landscaping, since we both had black thumbs. We were the furthest thing from gardeners, although Rick was very proud of the grass in the yard and would cut and water it lovingly. We were taking pictures in our minds of that future home, and we giggled like children. Rick and I had detailed discussions about what we wanted and what we didn't. We wanted our house to be a safe haven for kids; we wanted Macy to want to bring her friends to our house. With thoughts of a media room and a pool, our house was really taking shape. There we were in our old junky car, in the dead of summer like giddy high school children—dreaming. It was one of my favorite days.

Dearest Rick,

You truly are the most amazing man I have ever known. Somehow you make me fall more in love with you with each passing day. (I have loved you with every ounce of my being practically since I have known you . . . I guess my capacity to love has increased.)

Watching you with Macy touches me to my core. You are so kind and patient and loving and thoughtful and stable with her. When I watch her run to hug you or snuggle up next to you I am reminded just how lucky we are. You make our lives complete.

Our family life is so incredible as it is right now, it's hard to imagine it getting even better. I grow more excited every day with the thought of bringing our Caleb into the world. God has blessed me far more than I have ever deserved, but I am so very thankful every day. Our family is the most precious thing to me, and I will work every single day to be the best wife and mother I can be. Thank you for your continued patience and support of me. You inspire me with your example to be the best person I can be.

The upcoming months will be a mixture of enormous change and enormous happiness. I look so forward to sharing this experience with you. Even though it's kind of scary, I know everything will be fine because we are in it together.

I do so love and adore you!
Abby
see page 272

Although on bed rest for the last month of the pregnancy, I had been able to take Macy to her first two days of kindergarten. After those two days, Rick would drop her off with one of her classmates, whose mother would take them to school. Then one of Rick's students, usually Nick DeAnda, would get Macy after school, and she'd spend the last few minutes of class each day in Rick's classroom. We'd become so accustomed to spending our days together; staying home while Rick went off to teach and Macy went off to kindergarten was quite an adjustment.

Ab,

Just for the record . . . this spending 9 to 12 hours a day apart from one another is for the birds! I do not like it one little bit. I am so spoiled to us spending all of our time together. There have been far too many evenings of late where I was too tired to function . . . You are so good to me and patient with me. You are my hero for carrying Baby Huey—especially these past two months that have been so agonizing.

I truly never imagined marriage could be this good, this easy, this rewarding, this fulfilling. You are truly an amazing woman that makes me feel like the luckiest person on earth. I have said it before and will say it again—many, many more times—You are perfect for me in so many ways. You bring out the best in me and make me want to be the best husband and father possible. One thing I have come to realize is how much you lift my spirits at school. It has not been until recently that I have been here without you that it has hit me. No matter what went on with kids or whatever at school, it was all okay once I saw you, touched you, held you, heard from you—and I miss seeing you, touching you, holding you, and hearing from you all throughout the day at school. I never imagined this time apart would be so difficult. I have not always handled it well, I know. I am trying to enjoy the moments we have together more because they should be special right now. My resolution for these final 12 days of pregnancy and the start of Caleb's time here with us is to not sweat the small stuff, enjoy and cherish our family, and make sure this is a time we will all look back on with the fondest of memories. Thank you for everything—I love you and miss you and feel so lucky to have the opportunity to raise our two children together. ☺

R^2

see page 273

The doctors almost took Caleb early because of my blood pressure issues, but I have to stop myself from thinking too much about that. Sometimes I think if only they would've taken him a little early, it would've changed everything. I probably wouldn't have had chest pains that day. I wouldn't have rushed them out the door so I could get to the emergency room. Those little decisions that change the course of your life. But I can't go there because it's not my fault. It's not anybody's fault.

Doctors decided to wait and a C-section was scheduled for the last week in September. Rick and I could not contain our happiness. Still, I was scared to death of the major anesthesia and everything else. I made Rick promise not to watch the actual delivery, but he wouldn't have anyway. He was squeamish with blood and worried that he might faint, so he stayed right by my head the whole time. I felt intense pulling and tugging because Caleb was nine and a half pounds, carried in the body of a short-waisted five-foot-three mother. He had no more room! Dr. Jennings joked about him being a corn-fed boy, and we laughed.

Once he was finally delivered, Dr. Jennings showed him to Rick, who watched as they washed him and changed his first diaper. I remained on the table for a tubal ligation; Rick and I decided during the middle of the pregnancy that with two children we had our perfect family and would not have any additional children.

I finally got to see him, and there was this perfect baby. Cotton-blond hair. Big bright eyes just like Macy's. We named him Caleb Daniel—Daniel after my grandfather. Everything was going perfectly with recovering and breast-feeding. The lactation nurse came in and put on a video for us to watch. Rick, true to his personality, got out a pen and pad to take notes during the video, but we were both so exhausted. We were not thirty seconds into the video when Rick was sound asleep—sitting perfectly upright, head down, pen in hand. The man had the cleanest conscience of anyone on the planet because he could sleep anywhere.

During our stay in the hospital, I developed a slight case of "momma bear" syndrome. I had been so scared with Macy; I thought everybody knew how to do it better than me. But this time I was more confident and had read *The Baby Whisperer* and learned about staying calm and comforting your baby. I could comfort Caleb, and it was the best feeling in the world. He was my baby, and I knew what I was doing. I acknowledged that I was sometimes unreasonable while in the throes of my "momma bear" syndrome, but I couldn't quite fix it. I was euphorically happy, walking around the hospital and taking the utmost pleasure in caring for my baby.

We brought Caleb home in his University of Texas onesie, and it was a perfect day. He was such an easy baby. He was Rick. He had Rick's soul—an old soul. He was like a little old man and so handsome with such masculine features. He was very alert but with a quieter disposition than Macy. Whereas Macy seemed to attack the world, Caleb liked to sit back and take it all in. Macy was me personality-wise, but so much better. And Caleb was Rick. Life was heavenly once he was born. Rick was home with us for two weeks and was the perfect helpmate. They were by far the happiest two weeks of my entire life.

Abby,

Wow! We have children *now. We are responsible adults w/a minivan, two kids, and a house. Some days I am amazed at where we are. Other days I am just in awe. Other days I feel a bit overwhelmed. But* every *day I feel fortunate. Fortunate to be married to you. Fortunate to share my days and nights with you. Fortunate to have the rest of our lives to look forward to together.*

You complete me and you are the most amazing Supermom—EVER! No man could possibly have a better wife, best friend, soul mate, kids, or family life than I do. Thank you for sharing this life with me. ☺

R^2

—written October 10, 2006, three days before the wreck
see page 274

PART TWO

The Cocoon Stage

CHAPTER 7

Don't Bring Green Beans

Too many times we pray for ease, but that's a prayer seldom met. What we need to do is pray for roots that reach deep into the Eternal, so when the rains fall and the winds blow, we won't be swept asunder.

—*Philip Gulley*

I made the decision very early on not to expose myself to any details about the wreck. Officer Pirtle's words—"we found no survivors"—had been instantly realized as I stood on the side of the road that fateful evening. I didn't need to know another thing. Specifics served no purpose for me. The general information I did know was enough.

I'd been told that the police were notified of an erratic driver traveling over a hundred miles per hour and were en route to get him off the road when the wreck occurred. He'd veered into Rick's lane and hit them head-on. I learned that the police arrived on the scene mere seconds after the collision, and Officer Pirtle, in a testament to his goodness, assured me that my family's death had been instant. And that is what I believe. I knew they were gone; I knew where they went. I knew that even if there was pain involved, it was very limited and then they were at peace. That is all I needed to know. Luckily, God saved me from actually seeing the vehicles and etching that scene in my mind forever.

My last image of Macy is of her hugging herself in front of my car, telling me that she loved me. I can still visualize Rick standing by our counter and Caleb at peace in his carrier. That is what I remember. Some people may need the closure that comes from viewing their loved ones one final time, but for me, that would've spurred nightmares for the rest of my life.

Ronnie Daniel, the Justice of the Peace and a blessing of a man, committed himself to taking copious notes about the wreck and told me if I ever changed my mind and wanted to know the details, he'd have them for me. Still, after over three years, I have no desire to ever read them. While I am a strong believer in "knowledge is power," there are times when information is beneficial and times when it does more harm than good. Sometimes, Pandora's box needs to stay shut. I had to protect myself and only deal with what I could handle—to focus on what would help me to go on. The gravity of my loss was enough of a challenge. From the onset, I thought, *How do I get up from this? What is going to move me forward?*

After leaving the scene, throwing a bag together at my house, and dazedly riding with my ex-sister-in-law to her home, I stepped out of the car and was instantly enveloped in a hug from Max Callahan, Canton High's principal and our dear friend, who'd been waiting for me on the porch. Sobbing, all he could say was, "I'm so sorry," and all I could do was look at him. We went inside to a couch in the kitchen's breakfast nook and just sat, taking it all in.

News of the wreck spread like wildfire. That night was the Homecoming football game for Canton High; "Max" was the name I finally supplied when asked who I wanted called. He'd immediately gotten up to leave the game, briefly explaining that the Rike family had been in a terrible accident. The information quickly exploded through the crowd. Many people thought I'd been in the wreck as well, since we did everything together. As more details reached the community, the dance following the football game was eventually canceled; teachers and chaperones served as counselors to the students, who showed up to weep together.

In the absence of my parents and brother, our colleagues and friends came to the house in droves, their presence a huge comfort to me. Kristin Rose, the librarian at school and one of my closest friends, came through the house and grabbed me, unable to hold back her sobs. I sat there, in between Max and Kristin, with dry eyes; I hadn't cried out since hearing the horrific news with my mother on the phone at the roadside. My phone rang continuously, but I didn't answer. I didn't even know where it was. I only spoke with my parents again that night regarding their thoughts about chartering a plane to get to me as soon as possible. The risk of such a flight was more than I could take, and I made my mother promise to wait for a commercial flight the next day. I very clearly remember my mother's resolve that first night. Amid what must have been unbearable pain for her, she remained calm, together, and solid—an absolute rock—saying that she loved me and would be there as soon as she could.

So many wonderful people came that night: Betsy McCarty, Kim Travis, Randy Teague, Julie Murray—too many to name. I learned later that hundreds came, some standing outside on the lawn. I appreciated them all. Sitting on that couch, we calmly talked about Rick, Macy, and Caleb and how amazing they were.

I avowed that I was not mad at God. In fact, I felt God's presence at that time more than I ever had. I was never angry, and that didn't make sense to many people. But I knew that God didn't do this. We as humans have free choice, and when people make bad choices, other humans suffer. It doesn't make sense, and we can ask why God didn't fix it or change it. The fact is we do not have the mind of God; as smart as we think we are, we know nothing in terms of what God knows. In that moment, I immediately knew that countless people would be influenced by my reaction. I'd lost the only thing I valued: my family. Had I lost every penny I owned, my career, my health, it would not have broken me the way this did. How was I going to respond? Having faith when life is wonderful is one thing; faith in the dark, ugly, horrible times is on a whole different level. I refused to lament to God in a pitiful search for why this happened to me. In the kitchen that first night, surrounded by people who'd adored my family, I simply sat and absorbed the fact that it really happened. I never denied the truth that my family was gone, but I now had to realize a new reality.

Around midnight after everyone left, I was forced to deal with one overt sign of the motherly role I'd once held. With a breastfeeding infant, I'd cherished the quiet time spent feeding and bonding with Caleb. In the wake of my tragedy, the agony of having no infant to nourish was painful in every sense of the word. My doctor suggested I handle the engorgement by applying cabbage leaves and wrapping myself with an ace bandage. So there I was, in Walmart in the early morning hours, lactating. I bought light blue and pink fleece pajamas, a tight sports bra, ace bandages and cabbage, and did what I could to keep the swelling and the pressure to a minimum. To this day, I can summon the sickening smell of breast milk on cabbage.

My brother drove through the night and arrived early that morning; my parents arrived the next day at noon. I was still in my new pajamas and hadn't eaten. I went home with my parents to get more clothes and put on makeup; I saw no need to look as terrible as I felt.

Back at my parents' home, there was an unbelievable amount of food. I'll never forget the huge aluminum disposable trays of green beans. I thought to myself, *What in the world do you do with this many green beans? I have no appetite and if I did, it wouldn't be for green beans!* Whoever brought them did it with the purest heart, and I am truly grateful! But I didn't eat for days. I remember taking a bite of something and just not being able to swallow.

I hugged those who came and talked with them without breaking down, not because I felt like I needed to put on an act but because that was just not how I dealt with it. I did not want to be taken care of; I did not want to be needy. Nothing comforted me. I didn't want people to touch me. I could hug for a second, but any excessive lingering made me feel like I was coming out of my skin. I was all too aware that my only comfort, my only safe place, was gone forever. When it was all of us together—Rick and me snuggled up with Macy and Caleb—I had that feeling of safety, security, peace, and comfort. I had that every day. And without that safe place, I've been uncomfortable every day since.

One person who was a great help to me was Waunice Newton, whose husband baptized me at six years old and was my lifetime preacher. She had suffered through her husband's death and had lost a child. She told me, "People are going to say really stupid things, just be prepared." It was the best advice she could possibly have given me.

One line I heard regularly was "you have three angels watching over you." Humans do not become angels when they go to heaven. Angels are separate entities from humans. I know that people mean well, and when they see you in such pain, suffering such an unfathomable tragedy, they feel the need to say something profound. But the best thing to do is to listen—and to listen without telling your own tales of loss. I heard many comparison stories: "I know how you feel. I lost my grandmother." "I understand. I recently lost my dog." At this stage, I recognize that they were finding a way to identify and connect with me, but the best gift you can give someone who's suffering a loss is to say nothing. It's not the time; it's not about you.

Waunice also gave me an amazing book, *Getting Through the Night* by Eugenia Price; it was the only thing that really brought me comfort. Reading it that Saturday night at my parents' house, lying in bed in what had been my grandpa's room, I felt hopeful and peaceful. It helped me come to terms with one of my burning questions. I wondered, *How is it in heaven? Because if they can see me, they can't be joyous.* The book beautifully explained that they weren't sad because they knew my end. It painted an image of my family, cheering me on. *Getting Through the Night* became part of my nightly ritual, and I'd fall asleep reading.

On Sunday, I met with about forty of our students at my brother's house. I wanted to tell them that I loved them, and we were going to get through this. I knew how much the students had been impacted by the wreck, especially those who'd been part of our lives outside of school. Jessica Cozart was a junior the year of the accident, and, next to myself and my parents, she was probably impacted the most. At school without Rick or me, surrounded by classmates who didn't understand how close she truly was to us, Jessica couldn't express the fact that she wasn't just our student—she was our family. Meeting with the students, I discussed the memorial service I was planning for the coming Tuesday. It was going to be held in the auditorium of Canton High School, and I asked if anyone wanted to speak at the memorial. Five girls volunteered, and I chose to include all five. Jessica channeled her grief into a Team Rike memorial video, which she intensely worked on with two other students over the next few days. I wanted the service to be a celebration of the beauty of my family, and I took careful steps over the next couple of days to plan the perfect tribute.

I chose not to handle any of the arrangements for the funeral. My parents dealt with all those preparations. I approved of everything that was chosen, but I did not deal with any of those tasks directly. My decision to relinquish control over those particular plans was not due to any denial over it. It was about knowing what I could handle and recognizing what was and wasn't good for me. Planning my family's funeral was not good for me.

I did request a certain preacher who I loved dearly: Tim Watson. When I was a single mom, trying to find a church home, I'd visited many places where I believed I was looked at as trash. Tim Watson made a point to make me feel welcome. He was a wonderful man and very special to me; I couldn't imagine anyone else carrying out the funeral.

We held a graveside service on Tuesday morning. I sat in the front row with my parents, facing the closed casket and the pictures of my family. We'd elected to place them all together in one casket, the way it should be. There was a picture of Macy kissing Caleb on the forehead and another of Rick, Macy, and Caleb together in the hospital. I remember sitting there looking at that picture, and I could feel Rick there. I kept thinking, *I love you. I just love you.* The whole time I felt him telling me *You're going to be okay.* The picture was piercing, and it represented every perfect, wonderful part of his being.

We listened to the bagpipe instrumental version of

"Amazing Grace" before Tim said a few words. Rick's family and friends read their written pieces, and then Tim read the words my parents and I put together about Rick, Macy, and Caleb—about Team Rike.

He told the story of when my student Stormi James and I were in the library looking through our yearbooks, and she exclaimed, "Oh, my gosh! My mother!" at the sight of the enormous bow in her hair in her second grade picture. I assured her, "Stormi, all that says is that your mother loved you. You can tell whose mother loves them the most by the size of their bow." I shared those thoughts with Macy—that I didn't want there to ever be a question of whose mother loved them the most, so she'd always have the biggest bow. On her first day of kindergarten, I put her hair up in two dog-ears with knots and added two ribbons on each side— brown grosgrain ribbon and green sheer ribbon. She wore brown gaucho pants, a green peasant shirt, and a denim vest. She was an absolute vision.

Dear Macy,

I just wanted to write you this letter so you would know just how very special you are to me. You are an extraordinary little girl! You never cease to amaze me with your kind heart, incredible sense of humor, unbelievable intellect, and overwhelming beauty. You are everything and so much more than I could ever dream of in a daughter. I am so proud of you for the girl you are and the woman you will become.

You can never know what will happen in this world, but please know how much I love and adore you. I hope I tell you and show you enough. You have such an incredibly bright future ahead of you. There is absolutely nothing you can't do if you set your mind to it. You are a winner! My only desire or wish for you is that you accept Jesus Christ as your personal Lord and Savior and that you are happy. If those two things happen, then I have done my job as your mother.

I know that I make a lot of mistakes, and for those I am truly sorry. I will continue to work to be more patient and kind to you. You deserve that. I love you more than life itself, precious girl. Please know that you always have someone in your corner who supports and loves you through the good times and the bad. Never feel like you are alone, because I am always with you, even if only in spirit.

You have been the biggest blessing in my life. I certainly don't deserve all the joy you have brought me, but I am very grateful to know you and have the opportunity to share this life with you. I am proud to be your mother.

> *I love you to the end of the earth and back again,*
> *Mom*

After Tim's commentary on the indisputable fact that Macy's mother loved her best because of the size of her bows, he went on to talk about Caleb and how he was the only boy in the family, the hope of all that was to come. Tim reflected on all the fantasies about the UT games Caleb would have gone to, the fishing trips, the times spent with my dad working his cows, and the dreams of what it would have been like. Tim read my parents' words about how Rick had come in and been everything they could ever want for their daughter to marry—such a perfect fit into our family. After a few closing words, the service ended with "You Raise Me Up" by Josh Groban.

I buried my family below a tombstone marked with "Team Rike" and the names of each family member—including mine. Regardless of where I go in my life, where my life takes me, I will be buried with them. They will always be my number one. That doesn't mean that I can never love anyone else or that I will never know joy again. It is simply the truth that I have had to learn to deal with. The truth is that my life will never be as good as it was on October 12, 2006. The reality is that I will never be the same after a loss like that. People live their whole lives trying to find what I had; I had the dream.

Immediately following the graveside service, we went to Canton High for the memorial. Everyone was seated, and the auditorium was packed. God bless the twelve hundred people who attended that memorial on that Tuesday afternoon—the memorial for a two-and-a-half-week-old infant, a five-year-old little girl, and a beloved leader in the school—not knowing what to expect. Into an auditorium with standing room only, I walked alone, all the way to the front with all eyes on me—staring to see. *What's she going to do?* Undoubtedly, those in attendance expected me to arrive in a wheelchair or in psychosis at best. I sat as the service began and listened to our five extraordinary students speak. Katy Moore, although she'd already graduated and started college classes, had returned home just for the memorial, and she quieted the room when she calmly took the stage as the first speaker.

I'm honored to be the first of the students to speak today. It seems only fitting, since I was in Mr. Rike's first period class the first day he taught at Canton High School. He came into class that morning, just a big ball of nerves, and about halfway through the class he stopped to finally take a breath. And I looked up oh so innocently and asked... "Ya nervous?" Well, from that point on, I was a part of Team Rike.

I know several of you here today who do not fully understand the bond between the Rike family and us students, but in truth we all were family. I know it may seem to some of you that we would fight a lot. But that is because we are close enough to get upset with each other and still know that we are loved and supported. I know this extremely well as I hold the record of being yelled at the most by Mr. Rike—not an easy feat, I might add. In fact, I even succeeded in being expelled from all things UIL related; but by later that same afternoon, things were back to the way they had always been.

My junior year, I didn't have Green Days and White Days like everyone else. I had Green Days...and I had Rike Days. This was a special time as I got to spend three-quarters of every other day in the Rikes' classrooms. I learned so much during this time, and much of my confidence and knowledge comes from Mr. Rike. He had a way of seeing the potential in people—he certainly saw it in me.

One of the running themes through a majority of my speeches was the comment, "You need more sources." I realize that while some of you are wondering what an extemp speech even is, others of you have been programmed, like myself, to not believe anything without proper evidence. So let me put your mind at ease as I cite an article from *Omnictionary*. The name "Rike" is from Norwegian origin and literally means "of the royal realm." It was a term used to describe royalty and aristocracy. Personally, I can't think of a greater description than that. After all, we all know that Macy was a princess and drama queen all her own. She never seemed to run out of energy. As far as Macy was concerned, it didn't matter what you were doing, how important it was, if you were her best friend, or if she'd never even met you; you, at any time, were a candidate to hear the words, "Wanna race?"

I regret that I never actually got to meet Caleb. But I do own one-thirtieth of a second of his life. For you see, about a week ago, I received an e-mail with a picture of Macy and Caleb. I'm sure I wasn't the only one to get this photo, but it is something I will treasure. For you see, this photo represents more than just a moment in time. It represents an ideal—the dream of the perfect family, the visions of selfless love between a brother and sister. And most of all, it documents the lives of Team Rike. A photo cannot be changed. The smiles there will be there forever—just like the soul. When you look at a picture and then put it away you know it will look the same next time. The expressions won't change—nothing can bother them. Rick, Macy, and Caleb are at this point. We've held them in our lives and spent time with them, but now that they are out of sight, it doesn't mean that they're gone—that they don't exist. We know exactly where they are and the expressions that they have. Their souls have become like a photograph, and nothing can bother them. So while for us it may be hard to understand some things, and no doubt we will get upset from time to time, just remember that for Rick, Macy, and Caleb...it's all smiles from here on out. Thank you all for coming to show your support. God Bless.

—*Katy Moore*

As Katy returned to her seat, Bethany Stiefer approached the podium. Looking out over the packed auditorium, she began to speak with the bravery and poise of someone twice her age.

This weekend all of our hearts have been torn into two. On Friday night a tragic accident took place that changed our lives forever...No one will know how much the Rikes mean to me. They have done so much to accept me here at Canton High School, and it saddens me that people that are so great have to go through so much pain.

Two words describe the curly red-haired little girl Macy, fire ball. She never ran out of energy. Always playing hide-and-seek or tag. And the great thing was if she didn't know you, within a few minutes she would...

Unfortunately I never got to meet Caleb. But I do remember how excited Mr. and Mrs. Rike were, and many of us were so excited for them...

I may have known Mr. Rike for only a year, but for that one year, my life was changed. Mr. Rike taught me things no other teacher had. He taught me to believe in myself, and to never give up, and forever I will carry that with me. Now I stand in front of a group and talk without clamming up. Mr. Rike was the kind of teacher everyone liked, even if you were the type to get into trouble, you respected him. That was what was wonderful about him. Even the kid no one liked because he was loud and rude, Mr. Rike loved. I'll never forget him with his dress shirt and tie. I'll carry his kind words and the memories I have with me forever.

The Rikes have changed my life drastically. I thank them for all they have done, because without their love, I wouldn't be where I am now, with the friends I have. They took me into their lives and showed me things I needed to see. I'll always remember Mr. Rike, Macy, and Caleb, and I know everyone that was touched by them will. I love them all more than anyone could understand.

—*Bethany Stiefer*

Jessica Cozart then took her place at the podium, an uncomfortable arena to a nonspeaker. Undaunted by the enormity of her audience, she spoke with grace and fortitude. Her words were filled with emotion, but she delivered them with remarkable composure.

The next speaker was Lauren Teel, who spoke of her adoration for Rick and her love for our children. The crowd laughed and cried as she shared her precious memories of Team Rike.

Mr. Richard Rike was beloved among students, scholars, colleagues, and family alike. He was always smiling: he had so many different smiles. He had his happy, "I'm eating cheese or Two Senoritas" smile, his "here comes Mrs. Rike" smile, his "we're running late team, eat faster" smile, his "wow, you gave a two minute out of seven speech, at least you did your best" smile. All of his smiles were so encouraging, so inspiring.

Mr. Rike linked us all together. He could take the most quiet math student and the most boisterous debater and put us on a bus together. We may not have all gotten along, or understood each other, but Mr. Rike did. He seemed to understand everyone, and that linked us all together in a shared love for him.

...The impact he had does not stop here, does not stop with only the people in this room. There are teen-agers, adults, and students of life everywhere that he impacted. He taught us to hunger for knowledge, speak eloquently, and pay attention to the world around us. As competitors, we all strive to be the best, and that's a good goal, but he also helped us to savor the education and the journey that came in utilizing our full potential.

Macy Marie Rike was a beautiful child. So vivacious in everything, she was incredibly smart as well. She was the only three-year-old I knew who knew world leaders, and later the only five-year-old who could talk about Kim Jong-Il while doing a cartwheel. Even the most tedious one-act play practices were lightened by Macy asking if you were wearing toenail polish.

Caleb Daniel Rike was a beautiful child from the pictures we saw, and we all know how thankful Mr. and Mrs. Rike were that he was born. She was also thankful that there weren't thirteen children in her belly, as many of her students liked to joke.

Mr. and Mrs. Rike were the parents of Team Rike, Macy, and Caleb—our little siblings. So it feels to a lot of us like we've lost a father. But as any other family in the time of tragedy, we will keep moving forward. We will remember them all, and they will always hold a place in our hearts.

—*Lauren Teel*

As the last student to speak, Emalee Daniel chose not to use the podium. With her hair pulled back in the customary low ponytail and her neck adorned with pearls (as I instructed them to do in competitions), she explained that in Team Rike, we didn't use podiums. She commanded the attention of every person in the room as she honored Rick, Macy, and Caleb with her beautifully written speech and brilliant delivery.

When Mr. and Mrs. Rike moved to Canton, a little over two years ago, none of the kids knew what to think about Mr. Rike. We couldn't imagine how anyone could be worthy of our beloved Mrs. Abby. However, in a matter of two weeks, we had all fallen in love with him. Not only were he and Mrs. Rike good together; they were perfect for each other. Last year, in English class, I wrote a paper about the Rikes. I would like to share part of it with you:

"In math class we were working on complementary angles, two acute angles that, when added together, create a full ninety-degree angle. This concept originally struck me as painfully dull; however, as I sat, staring at the page, an idea suddenly struck me. This concept of two incomplete pieces coming together to create a whole, was directly applicable to successful relationships in today's society. Just as two angles combine to become a complete entity, the most satisfying relationships seem to exist between two people who complement, or complete, each other. Mr. and Mrs. Rike are a prime example of this concept. I have always marveled at the profound level of compatibility they share. They adore each other; they appreciate each other's good qualities, while embracing their idiosyncrasies. They have very different strengths, Mrs. Rike being presentation oriented, and Mr. Rike being totally factual. Both are brilliant in their own way. They are, in my opinion, a complementary couple because they enhance each other's strengths and compensate for each other's weaknesses. Neither is complete without the other. However, together they are dynamic and fulfilled. They are, in other words, soul mates. It is such a blessing for me to have couples like this in my life; it gives me hope that there is someone out

there who will complete me in this way. It takes hundreds of components, coming together perfectly to create this ideal match, but it is worth the search. I believe it is God's will for us to find the person he created for us. We could all use a complementary component in our lives."

Not only was Mr. Rike a wonderful husband, he was also a precious father. It was such a blessing to watch him interact with Macy. No other dad I know would come to the "hair and makeup training session" for his daughter's cheerleading team, and sit on the floor with all the other moms and little girls, trying to learn how to fix his daughter's "crazy buns." He was also so proud of Caleb; he was all he talked about. They watched the Texas/OU game together, the obvious rite-of-passage for any Rike child. Mr. Rike's extraordinary gifts also extended to his teaching and his relationships with his students. Everything he did at our school, he did to the highest possible standards. He prepared daily packets for the Extemp and Current Events teams. He made sure that the boxes were meticulously organized and up-to-date. He gave his students every possible chance for success. His knowledge of every possible topic continually amazed us. Whether we were asking him if freedom of expression should be valued above political correctness, or about Mahmoud Ahmadinejad's chances for success, he always had the answer. He encouraged us to be all that we could be. Mr. Rike was always so supportive of us; he never raised his voice, or was critical any more than was absolutely necessary. I'll never forget when Courtney told him that she had called Supreme Court Justice Clarence Thomas, "Thomas Clarence" throughout her entire speech; he just sat down on the floor in the middle of the tournament and laughed! His "victory dance" when his current events team won first place at a tournament will remain forever etched in my memory, as will his loathing of the "Siberian tiger" intro. Mr. Rike loved us all unconditionally. It didn't matter if we were last place in district or first place in state; he loved us because he just loved kids.

Mr. Rike has personally had a profound impact on my life. He and Mrs. Abby have helped me become more confident, articulate, and self-sufficient, all of which have helped me to discover my gifts and develop a plan for my life. He has changed who I am; I am a better person because I knew him. I truly have no idea where I would be were it not for these two amazing people.

We always said that Mr. Rike had the patience of Job, but now it is Mrs. Abby that is in Job's place. The other day, Mrs. Abby said, "God loved Job, and God loves me." As tragic as this is, we are all so thankful that Mrs. Abby is still with us, because we love her and we need her in our lives. In the story of Job, when disaster hit, Job's friends came and sat in the ashes with him; they said nothing, but simply held him and grieved with him. That is all that we can do for Mrs. Abby now; just sit in the ashes and hold her and help her in any way we can.

If the Rikes have taught us anything, it is that we should use the hard times to make us stronger. We have a choice of giving up, or moving forward, and I know that Mr. Rike would have wanted us, as a UIL family, as a student body, and as a community, to move forward, and become better, stronger people as a result of our sorrow. Words cannot even begin to express how much we will miss Mr. Rike and his precious family, but they can live on through the impact they have given us. Through every speech we give, we can embody Mr. Rike's positive, patient nature. By being class acts, like he was, we can exemplify his amazing character and kind spirit. We can honor him by caring for his beloved wife and seeking God in all we do. Mr. Rike was an amazing, kind, irreplaceable person, but he can live on through us, if we bond together in a spirit of love. Once again, we will continue to pray for Mrs. Abby, and be there to sit in the ashes and hold her. The impact that the Rike family has had on so many lives will never be forgotten.

—*Emalee Daniel*

Everyone was blown away to see the students speak with such heart and virtuosity.

Not one of them broke down. The content of their speeches was overwhelmingly meaningful and brilliant. Their delivery would have wowed any human on the planet. It was like watching professional speakers; they embodied everything and more we'd ever taught them.

Dr. Monaco followed the students' speeches with a wit and way with words only he has. Though Doc runs a tight ship as superintendent, what endeared him to me was not only his love of my husband, but his unwavering focus on what is best for his students, faculty, and staff. Max Callahan did the eulogy, and then Tim did the service, speaking from the Book of Job as I'd asked him.

There are no words to describe what we are feeling this afternoon. In human terms, words like shock, disbelief, anger, depression, sadness, overwhelmed, numb, and heartache in the English language only go so far to describe what we are feeling deep down in our soul.

But, as we come this afternoon to celebrate three beautiful lives, the lives of Rick, Macy, and Caleb, in the midst of all the emotions we are feeling, there is a word from God. There is a word from the God of the universe; there is a word from the God who created them, and who even loves Rick, Macy, and Caleb more than we love them. God's word to Abby and your family is this: "As I am taking care of them, I will take care of you. I love them, and I love you, and I will be with you every step of the way."

That's a hard word for many of us to hear this afternoon. Many of us may even doubt this word—that God loves Rick, Macy, and Caleb more than we do. It may be hard for us to buy into that. Some of you may dismiss that as "preacher talk"—just empty words that preachers say at funerals.

Regardless of what you believe today, or how you feel about these events, the God of the universe still says to you, "I love you. Even when your heart is breaking, and you are confused, and you don't know which way is up, I love you. As I am taking care right now of your loved ones, I will take care of you, Abby, Ron, Billie. I am with you every step of the way."

In times like these, it is sometimes hard to hear that God loves us. Abby Rike believes this. Even in Abby's pain, grief, and heartache, she wants all of you to know that her family is in heaven with Jesus Christ. Even though she is heartbroken, she wants you to know God loves her. God loves Rick, Macy, and Caleb. And God loves you. Job 2:9–10 (NASB) says, *"Then his [Job's] wife said to him, 'Do you still hold fast your integrity? Curse God and die!' But Job said to her, 'You speak as one of the foolish women speaks. Shall we indeed accept good from God and not accept adversity?' In all of this Job did not sin with his lips."*

It is easy for us to accept the adversities that come from living in a sinful fallen world. One of the things Abby would want you to know, whether you are a senior in high school or a senior adult, is that God calls us to be faithful to Him even when times are hard and difficult—even when we feel as if we can't take one more step.

Abby, I want to say a personal word to you and to all the family members. The thing that you have today that some people don't have, the thing that you have to hold on to—to grab hold of—is hope. You have the assurance and hope of heaven that your family is with Jesus Christ.

But the thing that has gotten you through this weekend, the thing that has supported you today, and the thing that will anchor you in the days to come, is the hope you have personally through your faith in Jesus Christ. All of us must have Christ as our hope! That is the only way we will make it in this life. The hope we have through Jesus Christ.

In our society, our concept of hope is many times related to "wishful thinking." We say, "I hope it doesn't rain." What we are saying is, "I wish it wouldn't rain." Or, "I hope this doesn't happen," or, "I hope that doesn't matter." What we are saying is, "I wish this or that wouldn't happen." We seem to use the words "hope" and "wish" interchangeably. Hope is many times equated with "wishful thinking" from our society's viewpoint.

But in the Bible, the Bible's meaning of hope is totally different from society's meaning of hope. The word "hope" in the Bible carries with it the meaning of: "Confident expectation; joyful anticipation; a firm conviction about the future."

Abby and the family and friends of Rick, Macy, and Caleb, the good news is this: If we know Jesus Christ as our personal Savior, we not only have hope, meaning, and purpose in our lives on this earth, we have confident expectation, joyful anticipation, a firm conviction that we will see our loved ones one day. That's the hope that the gospel of Jesus Christ gives us today.

—*Tim Watson*

The basic message was that I loved the Lord and hoped in the Lord, and I wanted everyone else to love and hope in the Lord. This wasn't a time to be mad at God. It was a time to make sure you knew where you were going, because tomorrow is not guaranteed. The choir sang, then we played the Team Rike memorial video of pictures and film of Rick, Macy, and Caleb, put together by Jessica Cozart, Stormi James, and Katy Moore. The auditorium resounded with sobs at the video of Macy singing "Hush Little Baby" to her tiny brother Caleb, only to erupt in laughter when she recited her special line, "Momma's gonna buy you a porcupine." Once the service was complete, I stood by myself at the bottom of the stage and greeted whoever wanted to come by, reassuring them that we were all going to be okay.

A couple of days after the memorial, eager to get away from others' watchful eyes, I retreated to my house for more clothes. Accosted by Caleb's stroller and the "It's a Boy" balloon, still untouched as though nothing had happened, I walked straight into our bedroom. I promptly collapsed on our bed and screamed. I screamed and cried to the point of physical exhaustion—finally releasing the guttural wails and moans that no one can witness.

The next day I saw the butterflies in my parents' yard—a brief sign of hope, draping me in peace and strengthening my resolve to move forward and find happiness again, to learn to fly again. But I'd already started building my cocoon.

CHAPTER 8

Filling the Time

Do what you can, with what you have, where you are.
—*Theodore Roosevelt*

The only place I allowed myself to cry was in the shower. I'd stand there sobbing, dripping milk. That went on for over two weeks. All I had was time to think. Lactate and think.

I did a lot of soul searching and had numerous talks with God. I had a lot to say—*You better be real. You better be everything that I know You to be. If You are this big and this good, then I'm going to need You to start bestowing something on me immediately!* I was a little like Job, a little sassy with God. Luckily, God has big shoulders and loved me in spite of myself and blessed me with immediate feelings of peace during those brief moments of doubt. It didn't take away the grief, or the sadness, or the hurt, but I was comforted in knowing that God was with me and my family was at peace. God's grace is sufficient when we allow it to be and lean on His strength rather than our own.

In those first few weeks, I filled the days by sitting on the couch in my pajamas reading the hundreds of cards coming in every day. Evelyn Addis, a teacher who taught next door to Macy's kindergarten teacher Susan Murray, wrote me letters of encouragement. She'd lost her husband seven years prior, and I felt her energy and her presence in the beautiful words she shared with me. I was so thankful for every one of those cards, and as the worst thank-you note sender, I had to believe that those wonderful people who sent them would somehow know how grateful I was for the heartfelt words I read for hours each day. It occupied my time and my mind and helped me feel less alone.

My mother and I spent countless hours just talking and remembering. She always had the perfect mother's love—unconditional. I attribute being a good mother myself to the example she showed me. She kept her grief very private to allow me mine; I can't imagine how much she must have been suffering, watching me in such despair. Day after day we contemplated big questions about God and purpose and grief—those big questions with no real answer. *What is grief?* We wondered. *When will the grief "hit"?* Sundays and nights were the worst. Sundays had been family days. We'd go to church or Macy would go to Sunday school, and Rick and I would sleep in and have some morning quiet time. We had family dinners at my parents', watched football, and just enjoyed the day together. There's nothing to do on Sunday when you don't have a family.

Nights were dark—when I'd really think. Nighttime was when I let my darkest uncertainties roam free—*does*

God really exist? Is there really a heaven? The answer was always the same resonant *Yes*. I wrote a little at night and read from Job and Ecclesiastes, as well as books about grief. Most of them did not apply to me. They mainly dealt with the loss of a spouse, or with the loss of one child. There was nothing out there that fit my situation, which is good in the greater scheme of things. Still, no other book spoke to me like *Getting Through the Night*.

Night was when the feelings crept in and the reality of the situation set in. It was the time when the enormity of my loss was most apparent. I'd think back to our dreams— obtainable, real dreams: the possibility of new lucrative businesses, the end of teaching and the beginning of my career as a stay-at-home mom, our dream home full of smiling, laughing faces. Every one of those dreams was gone. Done. I'd lie in bed and think, *Now what do I do?* What do you do when you had everything you ever wanted and ten thousand times more? In those last two weeks with my family, I was on top of the world. I would not have changed a single thing. Everything was happening for us in a perfectly acceptable time frame, and I had the perfect life mate to share it with. And then in the midst of reaching for that future, it just disappeared. Gone on the side of the road.

As the weeks went by, I thought of how much I'd lost in my day-to-day life. Up until that point, I had purpose. There was a reason I was here, a reason I got up every day. I had many different purposes, and I loved them all. My children were my number one priority; raising children to be productive members of society is a daunting task, and one

I did not take lightly. That was my focus, my desire. Rick and I used to sit and talk about how excited we were to see what our children would be, what path they would choose. From two years old, Macy proclaimed that she was going to be a doctor. Obviously kids' dreams change, but it was great to think, *What if she is a doctor? A kindergarten teacher? A dancer?* We just wanted to be along for the ride of her life, to get to watch her grow.

Before the wreck, I was not the parent who begrudgingly brought my child to gymnastics. I didn't drop my child off and go run errands. I was the parent who sat at gymnastics, giddy and happy, watching every move that Macy made, making sure she was behaving, and savoring every second of it. I still had interests and ventures that made me distinctly me. I had a career; I was a wife; I had great coworker friends. It wasn't that my identity was wrapped up in her or that I'd lost my identity in my family. I'd created the identity I'd always wanted.

I got to watch the best version of myself every day. Macy had every good quality and none of the bad. I took such joy from watching her enjoy herself, whether it was cheerleading or gymnastics or playing with friends or pretending, and as she got older I got to see more and more of that. Macy was just this perfect creature, and I got to be her mother. I'd see her with other kids and think, *I'm the luckiest person alive because I get to be HER mother. I get to be Macy's mom!* I basked in the glow of that title. I had the same sense of pride when Caleb was born, and I couldn't wait to watch him grow. Late at night, that's where my mind went—to all the unrealized dreams. To the life of no dances, no cheerleading, no gymnastics, no family holidays, no wedding days, no grandchildren. It wasn't that I just lost them in the here and now; I lost everything that they were going to be. Part of my grieving process was accepting the realities of the situation—not making them more or less than what they were, but being accurate in the scope of things. That is what my life was. This is what it is now.

Now, it was nighttime. And at my age, everyone was married and with their family. I understood it; I unapologetically spent my time with my family above my friends, so I extended that understanding to others. But I was lonely with no one to talk to. Nighttime talks with Rick were gone. Lying there, I'd think, *What is a typical day in my life now? What can I find to fill these hours? To occupy my time and survive so I can get up and find something to fill the hours the next day?* It was a vicious cycle of trying to find a new normal and come to terms with the fact that I was not in that van.

I certainly had moments where I wished I'd died with them, though I was never going to make that happen. I never had a moment where I thought I'd take my own life, but I recognized that dying would be easier for me because heaven is a much better place, especially when things are this hard here. In some ways, living my worst nightmare every day brought a certain freedom. I lived (and still live) without fear because I am ready to go at any time. I know where I am going in the afterlife, and I have great peace about that. If I could really comprehend how great it is in heaven, I might try and go sooner. It would've been easier to be in the van, but I wasn't with my family for a reason.

I never had another chest pain after that night—never saw a doctor. I may never know the reason. And sometimes God uses really hideous circumstances. He does not create them to use for His glory, but can He buy them back? Yes. This was not God's plan, but can He use this? Yes. I never felt that I was being punished or that God didn't love me. I knew I didn't deserve how great my life had been only weeks before; therefore, I knew that I didn't deserve how bad it had become.

I often went over to my friend Kristin Rose's house in those early weeks. She would go to the depths with me and grieved with me. She would listen and not rush me. If it took me ten minutes to formulate a sentence, Kristin would wait. She wouldn't interject. Kristin grasped the magnitude of the loss and expressed it in the most empathetic way. She was so wonderful about not interrupting, not making me feel like I had to hurry my thoughts, because my thoughts were so scattered. Kristin lived on a schedule, went to bed early, got up early. But she stayed up into the middle of the night with me, letting me sit and cry and just be. She never had that need to talk; she'd simply listen, instinctively knowing that it was the time I needed to talk. Very few people have that skill. I was willing to share my innermost struggles with her at a time when I was very guarded. I was extremely private and careful because I didn't want people knowing the ugly parts of me, talking about me, or thinking I was weak. I didn't want people to see me break down. I didn't want to be a stumbling block—impeding others' spiritual growth with an example of disparaging faith. The company line if anyone called to ask about me was, "Abby's doing fine." It was way too raw, way too fresh to discuss openly. You can talk about the scar, but you can't talk with the wound.

After sleeping in my grandpa's old room for a few weeks, I decided it was time to start thinking about moving back home. I refused to move back in until Macy's and Caleb's rooms were cleaned out. Determined not to live in denial, I was not going to have a shrine.

Three weeks after the wreck, my mother and I went to my house to go through everything. I knew that I could not clean out Caleb's room. It was too sad with Caleb. I struggled with understanding how to mourn each family member. The grieving process for my brand-new baby was different from the process for my five-and-a-half-year-old or for my husband. Caleb was an infant; he slept in a bassinet and hadn't spent a night in his crib. He hadn't been here long enough; his umbilical cord hadn't fallen off yet. He was brand-new. In his room were all the things that he was supposed to play with one day, the things he never got to. Those were to-be-had memories, and it was too sad that those items spoke of such loss. The only memories I had of Caleb were in my mind. With Macy, memories were attached to every single thing in her room. Every item spurred a story, a thought, a memory. I didn't want anyone else touching her things. I had to touch them all. I hugged each precious piece close to my heart. It took so long because Macy colored on everything, and her room was full of "treasures," as she called them—rocks and non-sense and crazy felt pieces she'd half-glued onto something. But I needed to touch everything. I sat and thought aloud, *"What do you do with all this stuff? What do you do?"*

My mother packed Caleb's entire room, willing to do anything I needed her to do. I wanted it set up as a guest room, as it was before his birth. The guest room seemed more normal to me than Caleb's crib, which had only been there for a few weeks. An employee at my brother's tire store had a family member who was expecting a baby and needed things badly, so I gave Caleb's brand-new crib and brand-new fireman bedding away. Vahn and Clint came to take down the crib and put up the guest bed. They did the ugly work, and I still don't know how to ever say thank you or express the gratitude that is necessary.

My friends came throughout the day—Kristin Rose, Kim Neely, Lauren Wycough. We went through every gamut of emotion together from laughter over recalling silly things Macy had done, to joy over hearing everyone's Macy stories, to despair over coming across a hair ribbon. I marveled at all the toys in her dreamy little room—my old wooden kitchen and stove and dishes, little flower rugs, and a gorgeous rocker. Everyone advised me not to do anything for a year, until I gained more clarity. I boxed up most of the things in Macy's room and gave the gorgeous new bedding my mother had bought for her, as well as her bed, to Kristin's little girl, Claire. The room that had once housed so much life was now so empty.

We'd made Rick a walk-in closet in the laundry room,

and that is where the majority of his things stayed. I gave several of his ties to the students for competitions. One of our students, Blaine, competed in one of Rick's suits. If I felt at peace about something, I could give it away and feel good about it, but I couldn't (and still can't) just take everything to Goodwill. I'm still dealing with it all, figuring out what to do. I keep telling myself it's just stuff... but stuff is hard to deal with.

Soon after clearing the house, I had to clean out Rick's classroom at Canton High. I found cards he had bought me and hadn't given to me yet. I went through scraps of paper, notes, thoughts, every single e-mail. I took great comfort and pride in affirming that Rick was the man I knew him to be. When death leaves no time to clean up, no time to hide anything, people are left to deal with what is left behind. I was so thankful to have shared my life with a man so good and so honest and so true. Having no regrets made the grieving process that much better. Were we perfect? Far from it, but our flaws and mistakes were normal and reasonable. We lived in as perfect an earthly situation as there can be. Mistakes we made were innocent, and we'd claim them, apologize, and move forward. We worked every day to be more considerate, loving, and understanding.

I didn't have to think, *Why didn't I tell them I loved them? Why didn't I spend more time with them?* I didn't have to beat myself up over *I should have done this or I could have done that.* I had no what-ifs. Despite my flaws, I was the best mom I knew how to be, the best wife I knew how to be. And thank God Rick loved me and made me feel loved; he did such a great job of communicating that to me. I also always knew that Macy had a happy life, not a perfect life, but she was joyful and secure and loved. She had a zest and zeal and a love of life that comes from security. I figured I couldn't have screwed up that badly to have a kid that great! We certainly didn't have all the money in the world, but we were never lacking in love.

I moved back into the house three weeks after the wreck. I was supposed to return to teaching after Thanksgiving, but I decided to take leave until after the Christmas break. I needed more time to collect myself before returning to school. I spent the Thanksgiving holiday shopping in Houston. I had money set aside in my children's college fund, and I spent it. I bought a huge flat-screen TV, new bedding, an entertainment center, a beautiful ottoman, shoes, and clothes. It was quite a spree. Rodney Neely and Chad Rose put up a brand-new fence at my home. I did everything that Rick and I had once planned to do in stages and made our home as comfortable and as beautiful as I could. It was a preservation of the feeling I'd had while dreaming all those dreams with Rick.

That holiday season was extremely hard. About a month after the wreck, I allowed myself to feel a brief pang of anger, but I quickly realized I had no place to put it. I couldn't be angry at the driver; he was dead. I couldn't be angry at God. There was no one to be mad at, so typically I was mad at random drivers. It came out in road rage. Many oblivious drivers got the benefit of helping me through my grieving process without even knowing it.

I didn't follow the usual stages of the grieving process. I never got the benefit of denial or shock. I attribute my lucidity from the beginning to my faith, to God's grace. I kept a sense of humor and often made jokes that may have made some people uncomfortable. If I heard about someone with breast cancer or an incurable disease, I'd wonder why it couldn't be me. I would not have sought treatment had I found out I had cancer. At that point, it didn't matter to me whether I lived or died; I was just taking up space.

With Christmas quickly approaching, I struggled to find an outlet for the anguish that grew exponentially with every passing day. I thought back to Christmases growing up when I'd helped out at Buckner's Orphanage in Dallas, and I couldn't fathom the idea of children going without on such a special holiday. I weighed the benefits of serving others in need against the danger of exposing myself to raw, emotional encounters I could not handle. I certainly wasn't interested in having a public meltdown, but I was ultimately intrigued by the promise that helping others helps you. Thus, six weeks after the wreck, I traveled alone to Buckner's Orphanage, ready to pass out gifts and guide parents coming to shop for their children. I told no one my story. I picked up trash, restocked gifts, and greeted people in line. One woman in particular had a daughter who was Macy's age. I walked with her as we picked out Barbies and stuffed animals. After four or five hours, I was completely drained, but glad I'd done it.

On my way home from the orphanage, I stopped at the mall in Mesquite to drop off gifts I'd purchased for my "angels." We'd chosen an angel from the tree as a family each Christmas, talking with Macy about how fortunate we were to be able to help others who didn't have as much as we did. That Christmas, I did it alone—intentionally selecting a six-year-old girl and a baby boy from the Angel Tree in Mesquite. Delivering my gifts to the distribution center set up in the mall, I felt compelled to share my story with the workers. A look of complete disbelief overtook their faces as they questioned, "This October?" They couldn't comprehend that I was actually upright and out Christmas shopping, but I had to feel like I was doing something. Of course, buying for someone else's children was my way of having some semblance of a Christmas with Macy and Caleb—my way of tasting a bit of that old life, even if it was just for those short-lived moments spent shopping.

I want my life back. The one filled with hugs and kisses and laughter and joy. The life with my soul mate, my precious, joyful, perfect, curly, red-headed angel dumpling, and my blond-headed, blue-eyed, handsome little feller. The life that was perfect.

It's been long enough now to not just miss them, but ache for them. It sucks to be the one left behind. It sucks to be able to shop all day and only have me to buy for. It sucks to only have my laundry to do. How I long for baskets overflowing with Rick's boxers and T-shirts and towels. What I wouldn't give for baby blankets and baby clothes to wash in Dreft. What I wouldn't give to hang up Macy's shirts so they wouldn't shrink. I miss them so much that words seem so very inadequate. I am broken. I am so lost without them. They were the best part of me.

And it sucks because I feel guilty when I think of one person because there are always two more to think of, too. It's too much . . . too much to grieve for. Maybe I just need to set aside specific time to grieve for each person. But that's so hard, too, because we all just went together. When Rick and I said, "'til death do you part," I thought we would be old. We had our lives planned out. We were going to hold hands and love each other when we were old and gray. We were going to watch our children grow up and enjoy seeing whatever they wanted to become. It didn't matter what they chose to do.

I know I can't know the mind of God. I am affirmed of that every day because none of this makes any sense at all to me. I was a good wife and mother. I was far from perfect but I loved them and cherished them as perfectly as I could.

The irony of earthly life is just crazy. There are so many crappy parents that have litters of children and then great, stable, married people can't conceive. There are so many unhappy marriages that last fifty or more years, and mine . . . the most wonderful marriage I've ever seen or even heard of lasts only three years. Or even material things. While we were married we didn't have the extra money for new furniture or a fence or a big tv. And now that I have them, I don't have my family to enjoy them with.

And then I have to feel so fortunate to have such widespread love and support because people have been so good to me. I try to focus on all the positive because I know it could be worse, but it's still so hard. I just miss them so much. I know they are good. They are better than I can even fathom and that brings me comfort. But I'm selfish, too, because I want them here with me. I want bath time and stories and crying spells and couple time. I want my real life back . . . not this nightmare I can't wake up from. Unfortunately this is my real life . . . the nightmare one. They are gone from this earth and they aren't coming back.

As I sit out here writing this bawling my eyes out, back there is a group of people laughing and having a party. I want to go over there and scream how can you be so happy when my family is dead?

Old sayings are so true: "Life can change in the blink of an eye"; "Laugh and the world laughs with you"; "Cry and you cry alone"; "Laughter is good medicine."

My heart hurts. I feel so angry inside and I have no one to be mad at. I have no one to hate. I'm just stuck here to feel all these feelings, and the person I leaned on and shared everything with is gone. The people who defined my life are gone. The people who brought me so much happiness and complete JOY every single day of my life are gone. The people who I lived for are gone. The people who made me a better me are gone. What now? What do I do now? What plan does God have for me? If I have to suffer like this, then I want my life to matter. I want to know what I'm supposed to do. I want to know my plan. I am shattered and I'm trusting with childlike faith that God will put me back together again. This loss cannot be for naught.

—written by Abby on December 3, 2006, at 1:00 a.m.

In the grieving process, there is a period of time where it is all about you. It's about functioning at the level where you are and doing what it takes to heal—doing what you can with what you have where you are. It's about taking care of you and setting boundaries. But there has to come a point when it's not all about you anymore. We are not put on this earth to take. There are times and seasons when you take more than others, but my predominant philosophy is that we are here to contribute to the world. After a certain period of time (there is no set length), there comes a point when you have to move from existing to living, from living to contributing. That became my most important pursuit.

CHAPTER 9

When to Hold 'Em and When to Fold 'Em

I did not ask for the life that I was given, but it was given
nonetheless. And with it I did my best.
—*Adewale Akinnuoye-Agbaje as Mr. Eko on* Lost

Walking away from my job at Canton High was
never an option for me. Abandoning my classes
and the UIL program would have left dozens of
kids without the leader they needed and deserved. The students were truly part of our family; we were Team Rike—
not your standard competition group. UIL wasn't just what
kids did; it was who they were. As a member of the team, I
had a commitment to fulfill. Countless times in my teaching career, my message to students had been, "Happiness
is a choice." Never had that way of thinking been tested
to such a degree. I felt that it was my duty to translate into
action the words I'd spoken so often.

Officially returning to the classroom in January 2007,

less than three months after the wreck, I stepped back into teaching theater classes, casting and directing a play, and preparing speakers for events. Rick's responsibilities were so great and his influence so far-reaching that it took multiple teachers and staff to fill the void. We were lucky to have so many who were willing to handle the program and the competitions taking place in the spring months. Lauren Wycough, my former student and a state champion in prose, was hired as Rick's replacement.

My workload encompassed classes ranging from Theatre I to Theatre IV, a theater productions class, a debate class, and my UIL program duties. Still, it was not a tedious or overly demanding undertaking. The content of my classes was enjoyable and focused on hands-on projects rather than busywork. With the exception of Theatre I, the more advanced courses were composed of students I'd taught before who connected with the subject matter and with me; they were accustomed to my teaching style and my expectations, so there was no need to establish authority or address discipline. The students that year were unbelievably kind, mature, and easy. I had zero discipline problems; they did whatever I asked of them. At a time when I was literally trying to survive, the kids handled themselves and their assignments in a way that did not require constant scrutiny.

My classroom and separate office at Canton High was every teacher's dream. The size of three or four regular classrooms, it allowed me to create multiple areas for students to utilize. Tables and chairs formed the "Lecture Area," whereas a small-scale stage and two dressing rooms defined the "Acting Area." I took special care in assembling the "Home Area" with two full-size couches, an ottoman, bookshelves, and greenery. It was a beautiful, restful, charming little spot that became crucial to my survival at school. Some days were harder than others, and there were times, in my advanced classes, when the students and I would merely sit in the home area and visit with each other. That downtime was when the kids could just be themselves, talk about their day, and relax a bit. It was a time when we were all hurting and needed a place to experience that hurt and get through it together.

I have no guilt about time spent in the home area, because, as an educator, sometimes providing students with a safe space to express their thoughts and emotions is just as important as imparting skills and information. Twenty to thirty kids were in my room on those couches every day for lunch, and I never had to remind them to pick up their trash or to quiet down. They were the most respectful, amazing group of kids. My classes focused on their work, but it was a relaxed environment. The students did not require strict monitoring, and I was in survival mode. They knew what I was struggling with and what I had to give, which created an understood calm in the classroom. I could not have survived those months without them. Still, I couldn't truly share my burdens with the students, although in many ways they were better than the adults. The students didn't say stupid things. They didn't know what to say, so instead of pretending to, they sat in the ashes with me.

During my maternity leave from right after the wreck to when I returned in January, a box was placed in the library where students left letters, cards, drawings, poems, or whatever they wanted. To this day, I still have and treasure each and every scrap of paper.

"Go Team Rike!"

So I know that everything happens for a reason but I still just don't understand how a family so wonderful could just get torn apart! I'm so bad with words and so used to you encouraging me. I feel so horrible that there's nothing I can do for you. I love you so much Mrs. Rike and I don't know what I would do without you. You've helped me in ways I can't even explain. I can't wait to see you that way I can squeeze you so tight! Even though it's hard I promise to pray for you!

Love always, Serena

"This Guy I Know" by Josh Helms

There's this guy I know
He was one of a kind.
He loved everyone and everything
—especially cheese and vanilla coke.

There's this guy I know
Whom I thought went to
Harvard for two years—
Until he told me he had
Just bought the mug and
Paperweight that displayed
The school's name.

There's this guy I know
Who always dressed in
A tie and collared shirt
That never wrinkled . . . ever.

There's this guy I know
Who always wore a gold
Class ring that I always
Wondered about, but I
Never asked him where
It came from.

There's this guy I know
Who loved the Longhorns
Even more than I do
And hated losing almost
As much as I do.

I know this guy
And I know his family
And I know that he has
Left us, but even though
He is gone, I'll never
Say I knew him,
Because I know him,
And I know that he
Will never leave us.
Ever.

Mrs. Rike,

It is almost impossible to express in words what Mr. Rike taught me. He was a great person that touched many lives, including my own. I feel like it was just yesterday that I met him . . . It was the Thursday before school started, and we had early morning band rehearsal. I was looking for you (to sort out my schedule), and I thought you might be in his room. I walked in, and was met by Mr. Rike. He then showed me to your room, and we went from there. That schedule change turned out to be the best thing I've ever done. To be honest, I really thought Debate would be a blow off class, but was I in for a surprise. As the first 6 weeks progressed I ended up changing UIL events. When I changed to extemp I started learning about everything that was in the news. I don't think I've ever met somebody as informed as Mr. Rike. He was like a newspaper on feet. It took me a little bit to understand the whole (R^2) thing, but I finally got it!

I don't think I've ever met a little girl quite like Macy. Every time she walked in a room she brought so much joy and energy to it. Whenever she first met me she was very scared. I don't know why, but I have that effect on little kids. But before long she was giving me hugs and showing me her cartwheels. Macy's little cheeks were always as red as her hair. I remember one day Mr. Rike left Macy in the Drama room while he went to help the CXers. It probably isn't the best idea to leave a young child alone in a room with Craig! ☺ The next thing I remember is that Craig had knocked down the bookcase curtain, and it hit Macy. She cried for a couple of minutes, then just like any 5 year old, she told Craig that she was going to tell on him. It had to be the funniest thing ever.

Although I never got a chance to meet Caleb, I just know he was the sweetest baby. For some reason I think he would've grown up to be just like his daddy. I'm sure Mr. Rike was the happiest man on the planet the day Caleb was born!

How God could let something like this happen to such a good family I will never know. God has a plan for you, and I hope you fulfill it to the best of your ability. People's stupid mistakes can result in tragedies, but they also teach us all lessons. Lessons which we wish we didn't have to learn, but lessons that are vital to us. We all have a long road ahead of us, the longest for you, but I have faith that we will all reach the end of that road. Whether it be a month from now, or a lifetime, we will find the end of that everlasting road. Your strength inspires me!

I love you and your family so much,
Andrew Wilson

Mrs. Rike,

Though I haven't had you yet, I had your husband. He was my favorite teacher. I remember this one time, he had on his "Longhorn" sweatshirt. Well, I am "Aggie" so we were talking about on the next Monday, he wouldn't wear it. He told me, "Ok, on Monday I'll wear an 'Aggie' jacket, JUST FOR YOU! Oh, and Taylor, you made a '100' on your oral. See you Monday." Those were the last words he ever said to me.

That was the kind of person he was. He was sweet, kind,

caring, loving, and so much more that I can't describe. I want
you to know, I loved Mr. Rike and I'm praying for you!
Love, Taylor Montgomery

Mrs. Rike,
. . . I just want to let you know if you need ANY-
THING let me know. Mr. Rike was always there for me so
I'd like to return the favor through you . . .
The thing that means the most and sticks out in my head
constantly is how safe he made us feel when Coach Kenny got
shot. See, I was in his class then, and I thank God every day
that, of all the teachers, I was in Mr. Rike's class because he led
us in prayer which made me feel a thousand times safer. The
only thing I regret is when he wanted me to join the UIL team
in speech and debate, but I was scared. He helped me have a
voice and now I am loud and clear. I'm no longer afraid to stand
up and give my opinion, thanks to him. He helped me develop
as a person which is odd because he came off as shy himself.
The thing that hurts me the most about this tragedy is
y'all were the kind of couple you only find in fairy tales.
When I would see you two look at each other in the halls, you
could see the love in both of your eyes, and it hurts me think-
ing I'll never see you that happy anymore. You will continue
to stay in my prayers, and I appreciate all both of you have
done for me. Your family will always hold a place in my heart.
I know I can't make you feel better with these words, but I
needed to do this not just for you, but for me.

As for Macy, she was a beautiful little girl with a big heart and great personality. I loved when Mr. Rike would come in with another silly story of what she had done or said the day before. He would light up every time he talked about her. I don't even know what to say about Caleb. I know he was a handsome little boy. I'm just so sorry. I just don't want to dwell on the pain but on the good times. Just remember, we are all here for you and we love you.

With all my heart and with many prayers,
Jenie Addison

FAITH by Josh Bennett

Faith, something that we look forward to.
Kept sadly by oh so few
I am one who has it so very close to my heart.
I know from me it will never be apart.

Faith saves people's souls.
Letting God fill up their empty holes
Faith saves people's minds
Helping them keep Jesus Christ their important find.
Faith lets us know heaven is in wait
Which saves many from making their own fate

Above all faith shows us the way
Which Jesus Christ helps us with everyday
So when someone asks you what is faith for?
Tell them it is to be with Jesus Christ forevermore.

Dear Mrs. Rike,

I just want you to know how very much I love you! From the first day I had you, your whole presence just made me feel so welcome. I just can't help but to smile when you smile. You are just so special and you and Mr. Rike have touched my life in ways you just can't imagine. I will always remember your "sermons" on different things. You have such a beautiful heart and you make me want to do good in life, mainly because you are a living example of how great life can be, even with just your positive attitude.

. . . When I think of Mr. Rike, the first thing that comes to mind is patience. I have never met anyone with that much patience! . . . He is a wonderful man and he will never be forgotten. He had such an impact on my life, I can't really explain it but the things I have learned from the both of you have done wonders for me. You should be so proud of little Macy. She was the luckiest little girl to have you guys as parents. Your beautiful spirits just shined so brightly through her and even though she is half my age I looked up to her. I remember you telling our Theatre class about her bow on the first day of school and what it meant . . . my daughter will always have the biggest bow.

. . . A hero of mine once said when I was laughing hysterically one day, which happened often, that "I love that. I believe that laughter is the key to happiness; I believe it is extremely important to have that a part of your life!" Well that hero was you Mrs. Rike, and you have given me so many words of wisdom, so here's one to you: Always laugh . . . believe . . . and have faith . . . and the rest will come easy. I love *you more than you know Mrs. Rike and I will never forget what your whole family has done for me!*

I love you with all my heart!

Andrea Jackson

Dearest Mrs. Abby Rike,

I want to start off with an apology that has been long overdue. When I was put into your class last year, I'll admit that I was less than enthused. Theatre just wasn't my thing. And I wasn't so keen on trying to put forth any effort the whole year . . . but as the year went on, I grew to love one thing about that class—you. This world needs more awesome teachers like you, who are obviously dedicated, fun-loving, optimistic, intelligent, and spontaneous. Never will I forget that one day in the beginning of the year when I was having one of the · worst mornings of my entire teenage life, and you noticed, took me aside and genuinely asked how I was doing. I was caught off guard . . . and it touched me. Even though it may have looked like it didn't sink in, I was so grateful for your kindness. Thank you. I will never forget that fifth period Theatre arts class with those crazy football boys and your heartwarming laugh. I love your laugh, because it's the contagious kind in which one can't help but smile and laugh along every time we hear it.

I am honored to be one of Mr. Rike's students. And we will always be his students . . . The first day of journalism was a rapid one. He was so excited to get us started, and I was so ready to jump right in with him. I couldn't believe that I was actually going to experience journalism in action! Writing for the Canton Herald *probably doesn't seem all that exciting, but the thought of my work published was thrilling! And he was there to make it happen . . . for me, for all of us.*

I have decided that I am going to put forth full effort in a career in journalism and I want to work for the Rolling Stone. *Mr. Rike always liked that idea. I remember the first news stories that we wrote on our own. I handed mine in uncertain of its outcome, but once it reached his hands and he looked over it, he said to me, "Jessica, this is good." I thought my smile would never leave my face . . . He made me feel like I could do it and succeed . . . From now on, anything and every-thing I do that is related to journalism, I shall do in his honor and in remembrance of him.*

Another great thing about that class was at around 3:00, Nick DeAnda would go to the front of the school and get this beautiful, red-headed ball of energy and bring her to our class. We could all just feel her radiance fill the room when she arrived. Most days Macy would wander over to where Lauren Monus and I would be sitting. Lauren would have magic markers out and be doodling in my notebook . . . One day Macy decided that she wanted to use the pink one to color her fingernails with. And thought it would be great if she could color ours too. So of course we let her, fully enjoying her giggling while she covered the tips of our fingers with Crayola markers . . . Another memory that sticks out would be the day that she lost her bouncy ball. Oh, what a tragic day! She was absolutely hysterical about that precious bouncy ball that she had gotten that day and it had fallen from the pocket of her backpack. Mr. Rike was the super-dad and wiped her tears and promised that he would take her back up to school where she could get another from Mrs. Murray. It just about broke our hearts to see her crying like that! She was so awesome . . . She just had a way with words like no other five year old I knew. And I know a lot of them. Lauren usually doesn't take to children very well, but she was always hanging on Macy's every word. This has affected her tremendously and she told me Tuesday that in the future she wants to have a daughter and name her Macy. I recently found out that Macy and I share our middle names. I have always loved my middle name and am so proud to have that in common with this precious angel!

On Friday before the pep rally, I was in Mr. Rike's class and he was showing us the millions of pictures of that beautiful baby boy Caleb. He was so proud. I remember when he came back from his "maternity leave," if you will, and was talking about the journey to the hospital and his adventures he encountered there. It was so cute the way he couldn't stop smiling with every word he said . . . It was truly heartwarming to see him so giddy and excited and proud of this new life.

As you know, Mrs. May has stepped up to take Mr. Rike's classes . . . She told us today that she wants us to excel highly in our UIL competitions and others to think, "Wow. Mr. Rike really prepared his kids, even when they had to carry on without him." She wants us to do great in honor of him. And we all strongly agreed.

You have proven to be one of the strongest women I have ever met in my life. Not just anyone would have the ability to handle such a terrible situation as you are. And you're doing beautifully. It's wonderful how you are using the precious memories to focus on and get you through the tough times. You are definitely a role model for me and many others. Thank you for sharing your wonderful family with all of us. I just wish that I could have had the opportunity to be in their lovely presences for longer, but the time that I did share with them will stay with me forever. They shall not be forgotten!

Much Love and Prayers,
Jessica Marie Carroll

Mrs. Rike,
    I just wanted to pay my respects . . . and tell you how important you and your family became to me in the past year . . .
    Almost daily (an every-other-day sort of ritual) Nick DeAnda or someone would get up at 3:05 and walk to the front doors to pick up Macy. And every other day, she would come bouncing in, brimming with her adventures from school to tell. She was just so exuberant. It never failed to amaze me, how constantly cheerful she could be. The moment she walked in the room, she became the center of attention. It was an attention she thrived on. Her races and cartwheels—she loved being in the middle of everything. She had to know everyone . . .
    Mr. Rike was so full of confidence—faith—in the people around him. But it wasn't a sort of blind trust. He was realistic—more of a "trust man, and man will prove himself to be trusted" kind of person. And, amazingly, it seemed to work out with him . . .

Last week sometime, we went to class and he had his laptop and projector out. Baby picture time. (We just smiled, and general laughter and teasing ensued. We all wanted to see the much heard of Caleb, but had to give the father a bit of a hard time first.) Mr. Rike sort of hemmed and hawed and said that, "You know, no baby is really cute when they're first born." We laughed and then he said, "But Caleb really is good to look at." Then he showed us the pictures . . . Caleb was his son, UT and all. He was so proud of him . . . He said he sat there, holding your hand, the entire time. No fainting or anything. He was so proud and full of love for all of you . . .

I remember unloading the bus that day we had District UIL . . . You and Mr. Rike took me aside and handed me a silver medal for Journalism. It was for "all my hard work" you said. For trying. I can't tell you how much that meant to me, after I had "blown" my events—at least place-wise. That medal is hanging in my room, where it has been for the past seven, eight months, a reminder of last year, and my first year on Team Rike. It wasn't the only material reminder of last year, though, for Canton High School. The District trophy was something else. Everyone had to touch it, feel it. Make sure it was real. It was the Holy Grail of CHS. That trophy was sacred.

Just like their memories will be. He was a wonderful teacher and an extraordinary person to know. I couldn't believe it when I heard the news. I still keep wondering when I'll wake up and it'll all be back to normal . . .

Mr. Rike was incredible. The way he could take such a personal and caring interest in everyone. He knew what was

*going on in their lives. He knew our athletic schedules—
something I can barely keep up with. Knowing him is one of
the greatest honors and pleasures I have ever had and ever will
have. Just knowing that someone cared about me that much.
It's a comfort in itself.*

*Macy could be something else all together. She was so full
of life, incredibly inquisitive. She had the biggest bow, and
the mother who loved her the most. Always. I don't think
I've ever seen another five year old like her. She was sunshine.
Running, running, and running. Smiling, smiling, and
smiling. She had energy and talent. You two were so much
alike with your expressions and attitudes.*

*Mr. Rike and you loved Caleb so much. I remember,
before he was born . . . I saw you. You were holding open a
door or something . . . You were a mother-to-be, absolutely
glowing. Your love and Mr. Rike's love for Caleb and Macy
spilled over into your faces and actions. It was obvious. It was
all so perfect, so wonderful. Everything was going well.*

*Your loss will be greatly felt amongst all of us at CHS
(and especially in Team Rike) . . . We are here for you and our
prayers are with you.*

Love,
Emily Sterling

During that time I joined Aloha Fitness, a gym close
to school. I had an overabundance of energy, as though my
body and mind were constantly buzzing. Exercise (at least
what I thought was exercise at the time) calmed me. After
classes I went to the gym, rode the exercise bike for about

forty-five minutes, and lifted a few weights, then headed back to school for UIL practice. I didn't get in shape (I was still losing pregnancy weight at the time), but it was a great stress reliever.

I put extra effort into my outward appearance. I didn't want to look like I was falling apart—for my sake and for everyone else's. I had never been one to go without makeup, but before I'd only had time for a five-minute face. Now, I carefully applied full eye shadow, eyeliner, mascara, lipstick, blush—the works. I never dressed sloppily before the wreck, but I didn't have the money for high-end clothes and shoes. Now, I dressed to the nines every single day. I threw out my comfortable shoes and wore only heels. The compliments I received were good for my morale; pity and avoidance were the last things I wanted. My look was my protective barrier; it was my way of saying *"Look at me! I'm fine!"* It was like the worse I felt, the better I looked.

About a month after I'd come back to school, a girl I didn't teach approached me in the hallway on my way to lunch. Lauren and I often left campus during that time; I was always trying to jet out of there as quickly as possible to get a break. My car I affectionately named "Betsy" was my route of escape. The student quietly asked, "Can I talk to you for a minute?" After meeting her burdened eyes, I immediately said, "Of course," and ushered her into my classroom. She began to tell me that Rick had been her teacher, and she was going through a very trying time at home. Her living arrangement with her aunt wasn't working out; she'd been shuffled around a lot and would

WORKING IT OUT

be moving again. With an incarcerated father and a drug-
addicted mother, she considered suicide as a way out of her
horrific circumstances. She told me that she'd planned to
kill herself the night before, but thought of me. She confessed, "I thought that if you can survive this and get up
every day, then I can, too." I hugged her with tears in my
eyes and told her how glad I was. I told her I loved her and
that she was precious—that the world needed her. She left
my classroom that day, and I saw her very sparingly until
she eventually moved away. Our entire interaction probably lasted less than ten minutes, but it humbled me and
affirmed that I was doing the right thing by getting up and
coming to work every day—by fulfilling my obligation
and facing the world. That exchange with her confirmed
that something good can come from something so bad.

Still I struggled to come to terms with having such
unwanted influence over the people around me. When people shared with me that they hugged their children more
because of me, appreciated their husband more because of
me, valued their life more, or found strength to press on, I
had trouble even absorbing the weight of the statements.
Overwhelmed by my own feelings of weakness and doubt,
I felt unworthy of such admiration.

In the UIL program, despite the competitive basis, kids
had complete camaraderie and helped each other through
every step of the process. I was able to oversee the program
without feeling completely taxed by the pressure of it all.
Although I didn't attend every event, students went to just
as many tournaments as usual and were very successful. It

was amazing to see high school students take such responsibility for their work and for each other; it was a testament to what Rick and I believed: you've done your job when kids soar without you.

Looming in the distance, my April 17 birthday threatened to derail my meager efforts to focus on my job and daily routine. I dreaded its arrival because it represented a slow progression into a life of being alone with nothing to really celebrate. As the day inched closer and closer, my students assailed me with questions: "Are you coming to school on your birthday?" "Will you be here for your birthday?" I had a sneaking suspicion that they were planning something special. The morning of my birthday, I called my mother crying, unsure of how I'd make it through the day. She counseled me to just do the best I could, so I dressed up, bypassing my makeup routine out of sheer weariness.

I arrived at my first period theater productions class to a room filled with decorations, balloons, flowers, food set out on tables, a birthday cake, cupcakes, an ice chest of drinks, and a Sonic Diet Coke (my favorite) on my desk. The students gifted me with a birthday cape, complete with a flashing button and a crown. They could not have done anything more to make me feel special and loved. But there was indeed more.

Lounging in the home area, enjoying my birthday treats, I watched as the students played a movie they'd made for me the night before. Meeting at Logan's house, they'd each filmed alone in the bathroom, conveying their own personal messages of love and appreciation for the difference I'd made in their lives. The video ended with a group rendition of 50 Cent's classic hit "In Da Club." (In previous years, before I'd met Rick, on our way to competitions driving a fifteen-passenger van, the song frequented the radio. Each time it was played, I danced and sang, declaring it a sign that we were going to win. It quickly became our team's "good luck song.") As a tribute to those early days traveling to competitions, the students sang "Go Shorty. It's ya birthday! We gonna party like it's ya birthday!" The show ended with the group yelling, "We love you, Mrs. Rike!"

I savored every second of that thirty-minute video and laughed and cried with them on that couch. It was one of those few times when I couldn't speak. How could I thank them for something like that? For loving me like that? How many people get to see such tangible evidence of the difference they've made in others' lives? Throughout the rest of the day, I wore my cape and button with pride, receiving cards and gifts and love from colleagues and other students. What joy I'd have missed had I stayed in my house and hid myself from that day! So THANK YOU Blaine Willis, Jessica Cozart, Shae Akin, Nick DeAnda, Bobbye McAdoo, Josh Helms, Bethany Steifer, Jessica Peterson, Josh Bennett, Nick Travis, and Logan Malone!

Soon it was May and time for the state meet. Assigned to judge a prose round, I was removed from the room at the last moment when a colleague notified Jana Riggins, my high school speech coach who now oversaw UIL, that her students' piece was about fires. She was concerned that, in light of the wreck and loss of my family, I didn't need to be subjected to the performance. Jana agreed and placed me in a different room.

In a prose round, six contestants each have seven minutes to introduce and perform their piece. Judges then write critiques on ballots and give a general oral critique while ballots are being tallied.

One of the contestants was a boy who'd selected a nonfiction piece about a man and his wife. The man talked about his wife and how he'd loved and adored her since he was a child and how he'd made a mixed tape for her. It went on to reveal that his wife had cancer and then died. Watching this boy's performance, I cried, tears trickling down my face, but I wanted to sob—out loud—like a baby. It wasn't just the content of the piece that brought me to tears; it was the brilliant performer and the way he read it. He really grasped the meaning and conveyed it; it was everything a prose round should be, to move you and make you feel like you've been on a journey. I felt so blessed to be in his presence. I wrote on his ballot, "It has been my honor and privilege to listen to you today. Thank you for sharing your gift with me." As a judge who can find something to tweak in even the best performances, I did not have a single suggestion. It was as perfect a performance as I'd ever seen in my entire life.

When it came time for oral critiques, I had a hard time composing myself. There at the state meet in Austin—where Rick and I met, where he proposed, where we brought our students—I was already overwhelmed with emotion and inundated with it all. It was quite a task to get myself together so I could speak. I began speaking about how important it was for each of them to realize that it's great to be a state champion and get a pin and be the winner, but the real prize was the journey to get here. I stressed that life is not about a piece of metal that's just going to tarnish. I choked up while expressing my thoughts, and I was so embarrassed. The judges at the state meet are seen as a firing squad, there to tell you what you did wrong. Here I was crying!

Once the tears betrayed me, I felt compelled to share my circumstances. I explained, "Look, I'm coming from a really different place. My husband and two children were killed in a car accident in October. I know what it's like to be a competitor at the state meet, and I've been a coach. Coaches, I know you want your kid to win so badly. The fact is that out of this room, there's only going to be one happy person, and that breaks my heart because the talent in this room is so overwhelming. Regardless of what rank I have to write on your ballot, it is my wish that you think back to every practice tournament, to when you found this piece and were so happy, to when you had moments with your coach and it all came together. Obviously you're brilliant because you're one of the top six in the state. The memories you've created, the work ethic you've developed, the experience you've had, no one can ever take that away from you. So don't let a number on the bottom of a piece of paper rob you of an ounce of joy." I saw others tearing up as they listened to what had become a much more in-depth oral critique than I'd intended, ending my tenure with UIL on a fittingly poignant note.

By the time the school year ended that May, I knew I was not returning in August. The comfort level I'd enjoyed with such a wonderful group of kids was sure to end when a brand-new year began. I felt I had honored my commitment, and I just didn't have the emotional energy to start all over again with new students who wouldn't understand the need for couch time in the home area and would demand the careful attention I couldn't give. I was in a place where I had to consider what was best for me and only do what I could handle. To continue on at Canton High was to live in the past, working toward a dream that was no more. It was sometimes a glaring reminder of what I'd lost.

Still, I didn't want to retreat to my house and do nothing. I decided to go back to school to earn my master's degree, a feat Rick and I began together years earlier. We'd taken classes two nights a week, and I loved implementing new ideas in my classroom, like service learning projects. Though I was never a very good college student, I knew I could do it because I'd done it with Rick. That experience together gave me the courage to go back and finish what we'd started.

On my way back from the state tournament, faced with a summer of nothing to do, I stopped at a restaurant in Gun Barrel City, Texas, and saw an advertisement for a free poker league. Rick and I loved watching poker together and had learned a little from watching the poker tour on ESPN. We'd never had the time to really get into playing, but now I thought why not? The busier I stayed, the better. So I became a poker player, and it was one of the best things that ever happened to me.

Poker is an individual game. I didn't need a partner; I could play as a single person and get out of the house for a while. It was a place for me to fit when I felt like I didn't fit anywhere. I sat with other people at the table, and I could be social without having to be so serious all the time. The people in the poker league didn't know my other life. They didn't know Rick. They didn't know Macy or Caleb. They didn't know me as a teacher. To them, I was Abby, the poker player. And I was pretty good at it. I played poker on Monday, Thursday, and Friday nights, as well as Sunday afternoon. My entire schedule revolved around poker—getting ready for poker, going early to poker, having dinner with other players. I eventually shared my story with friends as I became a regular, and it was a warm, welcoming place to go—a lifesaver for me at the time.

Through poker, I met Joshua, who quickly became my best friend and confidant. I felt comfortable sharing my story with him, and he weathered many tough times with me. With the kindest spirit, he listened to my writings, allowed me to cry, and supported me as the lifeline I needed in some of my darkest days.

Master's classes at Texas A&M Commerce in Mesquite started in August, so my poker playing was forced to the backseat. I fell in love with the school and the subject matter. All classes were night classes to accommodate students with jobs. My focus was Secondary Education to work toward being a curriculum specialist. I immediately felt drawn to Dr. Joyce Miller, an African American woman whose courses were so daunting students nicknamed her

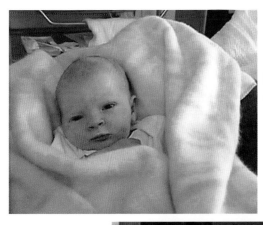

Macy, the day she was born.

Rick and Macy at the Aubrey house in 2003. Yes, that's Macy's very own Barbie blow-up bed.

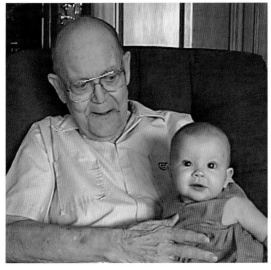

My grandfather, D.D. Day, with Macy. He called her his "Little Red Rose."

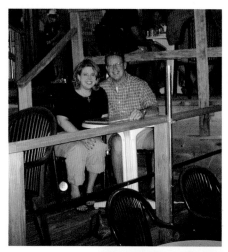

Rick and me at the Oasis in Austin, Texas, the night he proposed at sunset.

Macy, Papa, Maryl, Madelyn, and Gigi celebrating my dad's birthday on July 5, 2004.

Nanny Pat with Macy on her fifth birthday.

Macy twirling at
Papa and Gigi's house,
December 2004.

Macy with
Jessica Cozart
making a
Christmas
"treasure."

Natalie Whitehead
and Rachael Patterson
after the regional
meet. Natalie passed
away in May 2005.

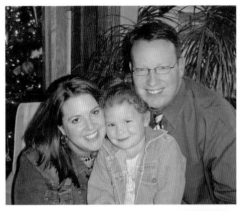

The Rike family, December 2005.

A speech banquet in 2006. I was pregnant with Caleb, and the students gave us a gift certificate and gift bag to celebrate.

Macy on her first day of kindergarten.

Caleb, Macy, and Rick at the hospital the day Caleb was born.

Rick with Caleb the day we brought him home from the hospital. Of course Caleb had to come home in a University of Texas onesie. We were training him right from the start.

Macy and Caleb hanging out at home.

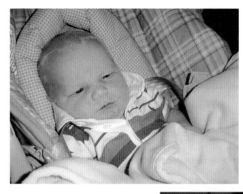

Caleb Daniel Rike, one week old.

Mommy adoring Caleb right before his first visit to the doctor's office.

Rick giving Macy a ring on our wedding day.

UIL kids at the awards banquet the spring after the wreck. These kids sat in the ashes with me.

Casie Thibodeaux, me, and Jennie Toups, hanging out right before *The Biggest Loser.*

Me with Christy Gregg the day we auditioned for *The Biggest Loser* in Dallas, Texas.

Brandon Roberts, *The Biggest Loser* story producer. He played a major role in my journey!

Kim and Rodney Neely—love these guys!

Front row: Madge Gautreaux, Amber Null, Larke Fabre, Tricia Corbin, Casie Thibodeaux, Gina Rhodes, Cindy Matherne. Back row: Glenda Deroche, Trisha Melancon, Becky Prestidge, Christy Gregg, me, Myrna Folse, Myra Stouflett, Winnie Pellegrin, Shelly Fernandez, Jennie Toups.

Me with my precious writing partner, Becky Prestidge.

Me with my trainer, Jeremy Allen, from the Tom Landry Center. This photo was taken while we were in New York for the *Life & Style* shoot.

My mother and me in Central Park after my *Today Show* appearance.

My brother, Daren; Gigi; Maryl; me; Madelyn; and Papa the day before *The Biggest Loser* finale.

Shay and me after hair and makeup for *The Biggest Loser* finale.

Evelyn Addis and me right after *The Biggest Loser* finale. Evelyn taught next door to Macy's kindergarten teacher and has been an enormous blessing to me!

My nieces, Madelyn and Maryl, with Jillian Michaels and me after *The Biggest Loser* finale.

Alison Sweeney and me after *The Biggest Loser* finale.

My surprise birthday party in 2007. From left: Blaine Willis, Stormi James, Michael Lawrence, Josh Helms, Morgan Cummings, me, Kelsey Shaw, Nick DeAnda, Shae Akin, Nick Travis, Jessie Allen, Jasmine Sockwell, Logan Malone, Jessica Cozart. Front row: Spider-Man (Bobbye McAdoo).

My cast and crew from *The Cover of Life*. Front row: Andy Landrum, Magean Thompson, Lauren Peel, Alli Green. Back row: Jessica Davis, Stephanie Sides, Lauren Wycough, Amber Falk, Katie Monus, Brian Clark.

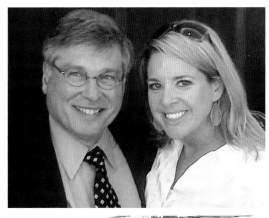

Dr. James Monaco and me. "Doc," as I affectionately refer to him, was like a father to Rick.

Vicky Vilcan, me, and Tammy Trosclair right after my first 5K race.

Emily Breaux and Daren, my brother. I met Emily at my gym in Houma. I introduced them even though they lived seven hours apart, and they got married November 6, 2010.

Michael O'Brien, Lisa Whelchel, Alicia Williams Garcia, Jennifer Rothschild, Sally Ann Roberts, and me at the Fresh Grounded Faith event in New Orelans.

Shelly, Sophie, and David Fernandez. They played a huge role in my moving back to Houma after the wreck.

Kristin, Oscar (the dog), Luke, Claire, and Chad Rose. They have been great friends of mine for years.

Marilyn, Max, me, Erin, and Lauren Callahan. Max was our principal at Canton High School. Lauren and Erin were both students of mine. They are like a second family to me.

Elizabeth Ann Batey, me, Gigi, Maryl, Emily, Madelyn, and Maxine (the dog) in the "Magic Room" having a tea party.

From left, front row: Brittani Engebretsen, Jana Sanders, Morgan Elliott; middle row: Nick DeAnda, Lauren Teel, Katy Moore, me, Shae Akin, Katelyn Deibert, Andrew Wilson. Back row: Brian Clark, Nick Travis, B. J. Waymire, Josh Helms, Blaine Willis, Jessica Cozart, Logan Malone.

Marc Danos, my current trainer at the Workout Co. in Houma, Louisiana.

"Killer Miller." I honestly loved her from the first day I met her. I could not get enough of her classes. I had a reverence for the life experiences she brought to the classroom. I'd not had many minority teachers, and her perspective was something I longed for and craved. Desperate to please her, I worked diligently and wanted her to think I was smart. She affirmed that for me, took me in, and I respected her immensely. She asked me to help with workshops, to put together a presentation, and to serve as a judge for an NAACP competition. Unwaveringly professional, she never showed favoritism, but I treasured her respect for me and for my work ethic. I learned so much from her and developed an empowering sense of worth and confidence for handling her classes so well. With amazing insight into the best ways to reach students, Dr. Miller shared my passion for true student learning and for imparting a love of learning while holding students to high standards. It was quite a task to focus on reading countless articles and texts and writing so many papers, but I forced myself because I needed the mental exercise; I needed to bring my mind out of its dull, frozen state.

Words seem so inadequate to describe the anguish I have felt. One thing I've learned is that grief, regardless of the cause, hurts the same. Most of the time though, grief is for a season. You lose a job or divorce a spouse, and as bad as the season of grief may be, you move on. You get another job, usually better than before, or you become a better person after a divorce, or meet someone else. But in my situation, I see no end in sight.

The devil got me in the only place he could really get me, but I'm still standing. Some days on my own two feet and others gripping the hell out of whatever is near.

So many of my ideas seem like such a contradiction. Maybe that's what grief really is . . . an oxymoron of everything. Sometimes my insides feel like they are raging out of control, but I can't lift my arms. Sometimes I feel dead inside, but I run until I can't go anymore. Sometimes I try to laugh at anything, and the tears betray me. There is such a fine line between laughter and tears. I was such a crybaby as a child that I try not to cry very often. Maybe I should cry more often. I have this need for people to see me as strong. I don't want to be pathetic or a victim. Deep inside though, I am very weak and struggling. Sometimes I think, Why don't people see it? How can they not know how lonely and sad I am? People avoid me. I don't really blame them. I know they don't know what to say. I wouldn't, either. It just makes for a very lonely life.

—written by Abby in October 2007

With the anticipation of the first anniversary of the wreck, I'd thought, *If I can just survive this year, what an accomplishment!* But then the reality of it all hit me square in the face. I was just a year older. And my tubes were tied. And I had no kids and no husband. This was my life, and I hated it.

As the holiday season approached, I couldn't imagine lending my services to Buckner's Orphanage as I'd done the previous Christmas. I couldn't think about even looking at a toy. With the passage of time, things were getting worse instead of better.

*I've decided that I am canceling this holiday season. I refuse
to have Thanksgiving or Christmas. I plan to clean my house
and organize closets on those days. I may even clean a toilet for
good measure!*

*This note may seem really random . . . It's just I have
been inundated with Christmas decorations everywhere I go.
I won't be able to shop for a month once the Christmas music
starts. It's too much, I say! TOO MUCH!!!*

—*written as a note on Abby's Facebook page as "Holidays-
Shmolidays" on Sunday, November 4, 2007, at 2:07 p.m.*

As part of a "mini-mester" in graduate school, I was taking multicultural studies with Dr. Miller. Inundated with
assignments and readings, I took a short break from class work
to spend Christmas with my mother and dad. Dad wasn't up
for a movie, so Mother and I saw *The Great Debaters*. Later in
the week, we visited the African American Museum at Fair
Park in Dallas, perusing the Rosa Parks exposition.

With school as my focus, I only played poker a couple
times a week. When the league disbanded at the end of the
year, I was deep into my studies and no longer socializing
as I had before. I'd enjoyed occasional dinners with Evelyn
Addis and Susan Murray, Macy's kindergarten teachers, and
developed a wonderful friendship with them, but in general,
despite every effort to maintain social relationships, no one
knew what to say to me, so they avoided me. I was lonely
and broken, but I always tried to laugh instead of being
somber all the time. I did everything I could to feel better;
I made sure not to complain or look especially pitiful, but

people still didn't know how to be around me. Eventually, those whom I did share things with became more and more distant, so I learned not to tell anyone anything. Nobody could handle it. Still, there were times when people would call, and I just couldn't answer the phone. Once I was ready to talk again, no one was calling.

There was a point when I couldn't be around people I'd known before the wreck. It was such a reminder of what my life no longer was. I knew they hurt for me and felt the enormity of my loss. They felt guilt over being grateful that it didn't happen to them, and fear over saying the wrong thing. The emotional baggage that came with being in my life was too much.

As the spring of 2008 came and went, I longed for companionship. I knew from the onset that I would never meet another Rick. No one was ever going to measure up to him; he was my split-apart. We were one. But at the same time, I was never so naïve to think that I could never love another person. I was a widow at thirty-two. With longevity in my family, I was looking at another fifty years of life. That's a long time to be lonely. I remembered telling Rick once that if something happened to me, I didn't want him to be alone. I knew that he loved me unconditionally and would have never wanted that for me. I was wise enough to know that it'd never be the same, but I still maintained hope that there could be someone whose company I could enjoy, whom I could love, who'd love me.

Nearing the end of my master's program, I felt a strong sense of pride for not falling apart; but, sans schoolwork, there was literally no one to call and nothing to do. Despite my polished exterior and my assertion that I was just fine, I wasn't. I needed a change.

I didn't like the isolated, sedentary direction my life was taking, and I knew there was more for me to do. I'd lived in Houma, Louisiana, during my first marriage, and the friendships I'd made left me with very fond memories. After visiting my friends David and Shelly in Houma that summer, I decided to submit my application to Terrebonne Parish School Board and let God put me where I needed to be. If Houma was meant to be the next stop on this journey, it would all work out. An hour after sending in the paperwork, my phone rang with a call about an opening for a ninth grade English position at South Terrebonne High School. Two days later, I had an interview in the morning and a new job by the afternoon. In the meantime, Cindy Matherne, a dear friend in Houma, tipped me off to a quaint little house for sale on Texas Avenue. Texas Avenue? Sold! And just like that, everything fell into place. Maybe moving would kick-start the next chapter of my life.

> *There's no way that I can tell everyone that I need to [about] my big news in person, so I am just going to write a note . . . Also, for those that don't know, I now have a myspace. =) (I posted this info there as well.)*
>
> *How it all came about . . .*
>
> *Last summer I visited my friends in Houma, LA, and during that time I seriously considered it a place I could live. (For those of you that don't know, I lived there between 1996 and 2000.) I didn't want to make any rash decisions, so I decided to*

stay put and go to grad school full time. I am so happy to report that I will graduate with my master's degree in August.

During my trip last week, I decided to put my application in with Terrebonne Parish School Board. Two days after I submitted my paperwork I got a call from South Terrebonne High School regarding an English position . . . yes, no typo there, English. (Another tidbit of info . . . I taught English for a year while in LA as well as applied algebra . . . crazy, I know.) The principal was out of town until Monday, so the assistant principal set up an interview at 7:00 a.m. Monday morning. After a ten-minute meeting, the principal offered me the position, which I accepted. So, I guess that makes me a gainfully employed individual again . . . =) I really want a master teacher position (somewhat administrative without all the extracurricular activities), but I need to get my foot in the door before that opportunity will be available, so it's back to the classroom I go.

Yesterday I placed an offer on a house in the Mulberry area. I am hoping to close before school starts, if not, David and Shelly have graciously offered for me to live with them until everything is settled. School starts August 5, so things are moving at a rapid pace to say the least. While I am scared to death of making such big changes, I feel like God's plan for my life is in action.

—written as a note on Abby's Facebook page as "Big Changes in Store for me" on Wednesday, June 11, 2008, at 3:56 p.m.

CHAPTER 10

Rock Bottom

What the caterpillar thinks is the end of the world, the butterfly knows is only the beginning.

—Anonymous

My first rude awakening came after I got the job, signed my contract, and arrived at South Terrebonne ready to decorate my classroom—a classroom that didn't exist. With twelve years of experience teaching theater (some of which were spent in the mother of all classrooms), I would be teaching freshman English on a cart, traveling from room to room. I immediately took stock of the fact that this was going to be an adjustment. Luckily, I had enough teaching experience to know that I'd make it. As I got to know the other teachers, I quickly became more at ease, especially after meeting Becky Prestidge.

Becky and I had an instant connection—she was a kindred spirit of sorts. Becky, at twenty-three years old, reminded me of myself at her age. She was a go-getter in the classroom, innovative and educated, and had a love of students that I admired. In addition to her work ethic, she had the kindest spirit and a tender heart. She and I bonded over drives to pick up lunch during our rushed schooltime. The way she spoke of her husband and children demonstrated a depth of understanding of the kind of love I knew so well. She listened to my broken heart and empathized in the most real way. I felt like she "got" it. I thanked God regularly for putting her in my path at a time when I needed someone the most. Little did I know she would help me put my story on the written page.

I absolutely loved the administration and the other teachers and immediately felt welcome, but the mandatory comprehensive curriculum left me overwhelmed and scrambling. Making all new lessons, learning new material, grading excessively, and trying to do a good job was beyond draining. My off period was the first period of the morning, which was great for planning but terrible for socializing. The students were ninth graders and challenged me at every turn in the beginning. After I used every trick in my bag to no avail, many students still hated the subject matter, refused to read, and class time was at times very difficult. By the end of the semester, though I was drained, I had grown to love them. The schedule alone was almost enough to do me in. I had been on a somewhat lax timetable for the past year; I didn't sleep all day by any means, but I'd wake up around 8:00. My new schedule began with waking up at 5:00 a.m. to be at school by 7:00. Classes started at 7:15 and ended at 2:15, leaving me with far too many afternoon and evening hours alone in an empty house. Through it all, I was the sickest I'd ever been in my life. I went to the doctor four times in one semester, running a fever with a sinus infection for five straight months. I didn't feel well. I was exhausted. It was a beating.

Then Hurricane Gustav hit in late August, and we had to evacuate temporarily. I went back to Texas to my brother's home and sat by the pool, enjoying the electricity and cable—unaffected by the power outages and damage caused by the storm back in Houma. I was on vacation.

Then came rude awakening number two. Because of school closures during the storm, teachers and students lost all holidays, and passing periods between classes were shortened from five minutes to three minutes. I now had to end class, pack my cart, travel to the next class, and prepare to teach, all within three short minutes. I was a day late and a dollar short every single hour and a half. The hurried atmosphere at work led to further exhaustion at home. I joined the Workout Co. in Houma, thinking that if I began exercising as I'd done in Canton I might start feeling better and meet new people, but I went very sporadically and spent most of my time at home.

With the passing of the second anniversary, I faced the stark reality that I'd been better the first year than the second. The second year was when I really started thinking, *This is your life. Is this it? This is not enough. This is not cutting it. I can't live like this.* I didn't ever give up; I kept trying, but the longer time went on the more I realized that I was just surviving—not living. I was the lowest I'd ever been, and not for lack of effort. I'd gone back to teaching three months after the wreck. I'd directed a play, started exercising, taken students to the state speaking tournament, joined a poker league, earned a master's degree, moved to a new place, and tried a new job. None of it resulted in a better life. I looked at pictures of myself from when I was still in Texas and was sickened—not because of my weight evidenced by my round face, but because my eyes were dead. It was one thing to accept that my life would never be as good as it was before the wreck, but to live a life this bad was unimaginable. Something had to give.

I'd never felt hindered by my weight; as an adult, no one ever treated me like I was fat. I was never left out of anything for being fat. But I was at a point where I had absolutely no energy to even get through the day.

So many people have messaged or left comments or called, and I have been really bad about responding. I just wanted to say that I'm really sorry! I appreciate your messages and calls more than you will know. The move to Louisiana has required more of an adjustment than I anticipated. Being in a new house, teaching at a new school, making new friends, though there have been lots of positives, has at times, kicked my tail.

Brief update: School—Our school STARTS at 7:15 in the morning. Since I live 25 minutes from my school, I get up at 5:00 . . . I know lots of people get up even earlier than that on a daily basis, but they are better people than me. I feel about a hundred years old at 7:00 p.m. when I think to myself, "Can I go to bed yet???"

Also, at my new school, I don't have my own class-room . . . I have a cart . . . yes, you heard correctly, a CART. I'm sure many of you remember what my desk looked like, so you can just imagine my cart . . . Between every class I wheel down the crowded hallway to my "borrowed" classroom for the 93 minutes for class. After the hurricane we changed our passing periods from 5 minutes to 3 . . . good times my friends, good times. Also as an added bonus of the hurricane, we have lost just about every holiday we were to have in the fall, including that we have finals on Monday and Tuesday, December 22 and 23.

I have also discovered that I am NOT an English teacher . . . especially not a freshman English teacher. If I am going to be in the classroom, I need to teach speech, debate, or theater. I don't know anymore what my perfect job would entail . . . I think I need to work with kids, but just not in the classroom full time. In Louisiana they have a gifted theater teacher who goes to different schools and works with gifted drama students, and I think I would love that . . . unfortunately someone already has that position.

On a positive and real note, I feel like the Lord has put me at South Terrebonne High School for a reason. I have even had several teachers tell me they feel like they were the reason I am here. It is humbling to say the least.

I have also made MANY good friends that I see on a regular basis. I have even had the opportunity to share my faith and love of Jesus Christ. While I am FAR from perfect, I see that God is using my tragedy to bring people closer to Him. That truly is our purpose in life, isn't it? He doesn't

*promise our life will be easy on this earth, but He does promise
His faithfulness. Though I don't know much, I do know that
is true!*

*I think of all of you OFTEN! I miss you all tremendously!!!
I thank God that I have so many wonderful people in my life
that I care about and care about me. Though I get caught up
in the happenings of the now of my life, I have not forgotten
about the people who helped shape me into the person I am.
All of you played a part in what was the best part of me . . . my
family.*

*Between Caleb's birthday and the two-year anniversary, I
hit a really rough patch of time. I felt lost and the saddest I had
been since right after it all happened. I contemplated quitting
my job and just moving back home. Through God's grace,
I got through that dark hour and began seeing rays of light.
While I am not fully in the sun, the light does give me hope.
Please continue to pray for me . . .*

*I will be coming home on Christmas Eve. Maybe we could
set a time, come and go or whatever, to get together. I could
certainly use a good outing to Two Senoritas or we would hang
out at my folks' house . . . If anyone is available or interested, I
will be free Saturday, December 27 . . . just let me know.*

Much love to all!

*—written as a note on Abby's Facebook page as "Sorry, and
Thank You!" on Saturday, December 13, 2008, at 11:10 a.m.*

When Christmas and the end of that first semester came
around, I was too tired to drive back home to Texas. My parents came to me, and I shared my feelings with my mother.

I was foundering. As much as I adored the new friends I'd made at school, everyone was married with kids, so weekends were brutal. But I certainly wasn't going to tell anyone how lonely I truly was, so no one imagined that I was sitting home alone with nothing but my thoughts. I knew that teaching English on a cart was not the job for me, but I didn't know what was. It was a time of great doubt and isolation.

> *I really think I don't cry enough about it. Maybe I just need to scream and throw a wall-eyed hissy fit, and I would be better after. Instead, I just let the tears trickle, then try to suck it up again. I don't know how to let go . . . How much pain can you really feel all at one time? How much loss and grief can a body take? This body feels heavy, and not just from my extra weight. I feel like I'm walking through the molasses of life.*
>
> *—written by Abby in January 2009*

When the spring semester began in January, I inherited a new grouping of kids. Now teaching Basic Composition, an elective writing course, I was free from the confines of a mandated curriculum. We once again had five minutes to change classes, which was much less stressful. I fell in love with so many of the kids that semester and felt that I was doing a good job. My off period now coincided with the off period of many of the friends I'd made, and I became close with quite a few of my colleagues and had some sense of a social life at school. It was a great comfort to have such an enjoyable group with whom I could sit in the lounge and cut up and laugh.

The administration affirmed my teaching and valued what I had to offer; I began to feel successful in the classroom again. Popping in during one particular lesson, the principal, Kenneth Delcambre, participated in a discussion about an upcoming writing assignment. Using current articles about illegally downloading music, the students were reflecting on ethical questions and reevaluating their stances. Mr. Delcambre thoroughly enjoyed the kids' reflections as they considered the difference between stealing a CD from a music store and illegally downloading songs online. Many students agreed that they'd never steal a CD but were okay with amassing scores of online music. We debated— does knowing you won't get caught make you any less of a thief? Similar success continued over the next few months, and I truly enjoyed class time that spring semester, feeding on the administration's positive reinforcement and the students' interest in the material.

Looking to better employ my master's degree with a job as a curriculum specialist, I applied for an opening at an elementary school in Terrebonne Parish. I did well in my interviews but had no background in elementary education; I was not the right person for the job. Still, I'd come highly recommended by the administration at South Terrebonne, and I knew I'd been given a fair shot at the position. It wasn't the right fit for me, and I was left still feeling the need to do something different—to try something new.

In January 2009, during one of my very infrequent visits to the gym, I ran into Brady and Vicky Vilcan, contestants from season six of *The Biggest Loser*. Thrilled to have met them, I quickly subscribed to Vicky's online blog and received the information that casting for season eight of *The Biggest Loser* had begun.

In the spring of 2007, I had read a book by Jen Lancaster describing her hilarious experience applying for the show. Thinking I could use a distraction in my life, I seriously considered auditioning for season six of the show, going so far as to find a partner only to later chicken out. The audition date turned out to be July 19, my wedding anniversary. I quickly realized I was in no way ready at that point in my life.

Though I had a job and kept busy for parts of each day, I still came home and sat alone every night. A weekly coffee date with my friends Jennie Toups and Casie Rhodes notwithstanding, I had few social outings. I was also blessed to have Cindy Matherne, who'd been a constant in my life since I'd first lived in Houma over eight years earlier. Though I never let her know just how much I was struggling mentally and emotionally, I greatly enjoyed our dinners together. Still, too many weekends consisted of me coming in at 3:00 on Friday afternoons and remaining sequestered in my house until Monday morning. I was so tired. I had no desire to go out—no desire to socialize, no desire to do anything. I would just sit at home in my cocoon and try to find energy. I was too private, or maybe prideful, to tell anyone how pathetic I was feeling, so it became a pattern of trying to regroup enough during the weekends to make it through the week. It was no way to live.

Friday, February 13, 2009, was a particularly dark and ugly day. It was exactly two and a half years since the wreck and the day before Valentine's Day. Sitting at home, my mind regressed to a time when every day was a celebration of love.

Anyone who really knows me, knows I'm not into cheesy Valentine's Day gifts. Red roses—copout... Traditional cards—weak... Candy—pffft... Rick and I laughed about such public displays. We decided the best part of Valentine's Day was that we didn't need a "special" day to tell each other how we felt. Rick was notorious for slipping a card in my desk on a random Tuesday. Frankly, I had zero expectations for any type of gift because it was just another day... another day in our perfect marriage.

Rick, being the man he was, couldn't just let the day pass. He made me a coupon book of all sorts of things... a shopping spree to Ross and Marshall's (we were on a budget), a weekend in Dallas (using our free Marriott points), unloading the dishwasher, and various other incredibly thoughtful things. Then he cut out hearts (or maybe got some students to) and put them all over our house. Each had a different message... I found some I had never seen before when I was cleaning out rooms...

We used to say we were the luckiest people on earth... we were...

—*written as a note on Abby's Facebook page as "Best Valentine's Day Memory" on Sunday, February 14, 2009*

It was all too much as I sat there and thought, *Time is supposed to make this better, easier, softer. Instead, time is just a spotlight on the unavoidable fact that I am completely and utterly alone.* For the longest time, I didn't bother calling anyone because experience had taught me not to share my lowest moments or people would avoid me. I learned not to place that burden on others. I usually protected myself by not calling or talking to anyone, because that way, they couldn't reject me. To seek someone out and get evasion in return seemed unbearable. Yet, on Friday, February 13, I was feeling so low, I was willing to take that chance. I called someone. It rang and rang until I left a message. I called someone else. It rang and rang; I left a message. After waiting and never getting a return call, I sat in that desolate state and thought about the information I'd gotten from Vicky the night before about auditions for *The Biggest Loser.*

I called my mother crying, lamenting, "It can't be this bad forever. I can't do this for the next fifty years!" I told her about *The Biggest Loser* audition, and she supported me as always. We both had our reservations (to say the least) about baring not only my body but my soul to the world. She knew how modest and private I was, but I needed to do something drastic to keep from succumbing to seclusion and despair. I later learned she thought I was completely crazy! I needed to give God the opportunity to guide my life, and auditioning gave me something different to do and focus on. I rectified the idea of wearing less than adequate clothing on national television by admitting that, despite adorning myself with beautiful outfits and makeup, everyone knew I was fat. I wasn't hiding it; it was no secret. Still, exposing my physical and emotional self to the world was a source of great anxiety. After getting my mother on board, I shared my plans with my friends at South Terrebonne on Monday. They showed such blind support and love, so positive and confident that I'd be chosen, not realizing the immense amount of people that apply and the slim-to-none chance of getting picked. My friend and fellow teacher Christy Gregg decided to apply with me, and we flew to the audition together.

On the plane to Dallas the next day at the break of dawn, Christy and I had our first opportunity to release our pent-up emotion. Neither of us being frequent travelers, upon hearing the awful noise of the landing gear closing after the ascent, we were frightened beyond all logic and began laughing to the point of tears. Our unfounded anxiety proved to be just that, and soon we'd landed and were heading to the audition. Arriving on site, we sat around a table to spill our stories in the hopes of getting the opportunity of a lifetime. Each interview lasted forty-five seconds to a minute, so when it was my turn, I kept it simple.

"My name is Abby. I am thirty-four years old. I normally don't introduce myself this way, but my husband and two children were killed in a car accident two and a half years ago."

I teared up and took a moment to compose myself.

"I decided very early on that I was going to live. And now I want to live better."

I went on to explain my attempts to carry on—getting my master's degree, moving and getting a new job—but it wasn't enough and I needed a change.

Everyone loves to play the "oneupsman" game regarding who has it harder in this life. What's really sad is when your life story wins. Whenever anyone hears my story I think they become immediately grateful that it isn't theirs. Sad. But deep down I don't really believe that to be true. Lots of times I see people around me, and I think I'm better off than they are because I still have hope and a future. Not the future I wanted, but deep down, way down, in places I can't put my finger on, there is a grain of hope. I cling to that grain.

—written by Abby in September 2007

We were told that if we'd been selected for the next round, we'd get a call Saturday night. My parents, Christy, and I were like junior high school girls, waiting for the boy to call. When the call didn't come, only slightly disappointed, we flew back Sunday feeling that we'd had a fun trip if nothing else. Sunday night I was at home, in a deep sleep, when my phone rang. I awoke to Holland Striplin from *The Biggest Loser* casting department, telling me I'd been called back for another interview. What I thought would be a phone interview was actually going to take place in person in Dallas. I was off to the races.

At work Monday, I made arrangements for my classes and prepared to drive to Dallas that afternoon for my next interview on Tuesday.

While waiting for the interview, I met a woman also going for her second interview. Rita Spires Jones became a safe place for me to be real. I barely knew her, but she had the most beautiful spirit. She had lost her mother and father; we had a great connection and talked about the anguish I

/ 2222222

felt. She was so encouraging and a godsend for me at the time. Sometimes it's easier to share with people removed from your life.

After my hour-long wait, my session ran thirty minutes past the allotted forty-five minutes, and I felt that it had gone well.

To fulfill further application requirements, I worked on a video with past students in Canton the next day before driving back to Houma. School on Thursday and Friday rounded out the frenzied week. The rest of my experience was very much a hurry-up-and-wait process: I answered questions, sent in writings and videotapes, then waited. I'd make it to the next round then wait. Still, it was something to be excited about and talk about in the lounge with friends. It was a great distraction from day-to-day drudgery and a prospect that something else was out there for me. I had no anxiety about not making it on the show; I just trusted that if this was the next step in my life, it would fall into place.

By this time my students knew I was auditioning for *The Biggest Loser,* and there might be a chance I wouldn't be returning to school after spring break. So two weeks before my actual birthday, my Basic Composition students made signs and threw me a surprise birthday party. It was during the party that I got the call that I had made it to finals and would be flying out to Los Angeles.

I headed out west full of anticipation and enormous faith, traveling to a world I knew nothing about. Living in a hotel room, waiting to hear a definitive answer about my spot on the show, I almost backed out. I was nearly paralyzed with fear until that nagging voice inside asked, *Since when have you let being scared of something keep you from following through? It's one thing to feel afraid. It's another to let it keep you from acting.*

The stress of this process is not for the faint of heart. The reality of it all is hitting me like a ton of bricks. I go from being terrified I won't be picked to being terrified that I will be picked. Am I strong enough to last at the ranch? Can I REALLY work out for 6 to 8 hours a day? Honestly, I don't know. I'd like to think I can do anything . . . I try not to stress about it, but it's consuming me. My face is breaking out, my stomach is OUT OF CONTROL, and I've sat at this computer crying for the past two hours. The reality of it all is that I miss my family . . . in particular Rick for this situation. How I long for his voice of reason and unwavering kindness and support. I know I would have never applied for the show had there been no accident, but I would love his advice right about now. I think it's the uncertainty of my future . . . yet again. I'm the girl who reads the last chapter of the book first so I can enjoy the rest. It's like I have to know what's going to happen at the end so I can enjoy the journey of the book. Life doesn't work like that so much . . . How I wish I knew my end. If I could look down the road, I would. Regardless of what the future holds, I would just like to know. I guess that's where faith comes in. I do have faith. I really do . . . I'm just human, and it's wavering a bit now. For so long I wanted what I had, and now I don't. I want more. Is that wrong or bad? I don't know. I feel like I don't know anything right now. Everyone thinks I'm getting on the show. I know they are just being supportive, but it's a big deal to get on the show. I thought about 25,000 people applied, but now I'm hearing somewhere in the neighborhood of 100,000+ people have applied. It's really flattering to have made it this far, but it would also really suck to make it this far, then not make it on the ranch. I like to win... at everything.

I guess I thought when I moved to Houma it would be a fresh start. Maybe it just hasn't lived up to my expectations. I still miss my family, I'm still really lonely, and I still feel like I have no purpose or direction. I do think I was supposed to be here this year for whatever reason. I just have no idea what it is.

Why do I do this to myself??? Why do I continually put myself out there??? Maybe I'm a sadist or just a glutton for punishment. But without great risk, there is no great reward. I completely put myself out there with Rick, and it was so worth it... it was just too short... way too short. Words seem so inadequate to communicate the pain in my soul right now. Words seem so trite. I wish I could write so that the magnitude of the grief was done justice. I feel like a boat with no rudder flailing around in the stormiest of seas... oh, yeah, and I forgot my life preserver. I pray right now for God to calm those seas and grant me the peace that passes all understanding. I have no control over anything... I am in His hands. Dear Lord, I pray You take all this nonsense and make of it what You will. Your will be done, not mine. How hard that is to pray. I claim Your promise that joy comes in the morning. Please hasten morning!!!

—written by Abby on March 30, 2009

Still suffering uncertainty, I answered a phone call from Bob Harper on May 11, 2009, announcing that I was officially on season eight of *The Biggest Loser!* I reacted with mixed emotions. Other than some mild aspirations of appearing on *Oprah*—as I'm sure every Oprah fan has—I'd never dreamed that television would be the avenue through which people heard my story and my message. At that time I didn't even know what my message or my purpose was!

As silly as it may sound, watching an Oprah *show inspires me more than just about anything. So many of her shows speak to me because she features people who are not only interesting, but have depth as well. I thought Rick and I might be featured one day for having the greatest love story of all time. I saw the show with the Holocaust survivors, and though their love story was beautiful, I didn't envy them because I knew what it was to love like that . . . I just didn't have that many years.*

Rick and I thought of sending in a tape of Macy quoting her world leaders at age three. We knew that there was no child as brilliant or beautiful as our Macy. Oprah has featured some phenomenal kids over the years, but none compared to Macy.

Now as I sit here in the quiet, I think I will sit on Oprah's couch as one of her featured survivors. I hope that my journey may possibly inspire or give hope to even one person. You see, there is no reason for my life if not to serve others. Everything that mattered at all has been taken from me. I don't much care for money or fame . . . purpose is what I seek. Why did God leave me behind?

—*written March 2009*

I was at a point where I thought, *Okay. I've failed. I've tried. Nothing's working.* I thought that maybe if I physically felt better, emotional health would follow. My choice to apply for *The Biggest Loser* was never about aesthetics. It was certainly not my desire to stand on a scale in a sports bra and spandex with my weight blaring for the entire world to see. It was the antithesis of everything I'd done up to that point. The show was not private. The show would not allow me to pretend that everything was fine. And I was convinced that the tender parts of me needed protection; I wanted to close the door and stay inside.

I had to come to grips with the fact that my cocoon was not the safe place. The cocoon was the suffocating place, the place where my vicious cycle continued and I asked, *Why is there no light? Why am I stuck here?* without ever actually finding an answer. The cocoon was tight and uncomfortable, not safe and inviting—a trap, not a haven. And the more I wrapped myself in layers and layers of protective coating, the harder it was to emerge from that false sense of security. It was not until later that I realized a cocoon is not a sweet escape from life. It is the absence of life.

PART THREE

The Butterfly Stage

CHAPTER 11

Treading Water

Faith is deliberate confidence in the character of God whose ways you may not understand at the time.

—Oswald Chambers

The last Diet Coke in my hotel refrigerator called my name as I furiously munched on lettuce and thought, *What was I thinking? What have I gotten myself into?* After stocking up on Diet Coke and ice cream during a trip to the grocery store, I was ready to treat myself to a few last hurrahs. A meeting with Cheryl Forberg, *The Biggest Loser* nutritionist, snapped me back to reality. While undergoing various tests and getting fitted for clothes, socks, and shoes, we were expected to begin eating better, a concept that sent me right back to the grocery store for healthier options and far away from that beckoning Diet Coke.

Through all the preliminary preparations before actual filming began, contestants were cut off from communication with the outside world (friends and family) and were not allowed to speak to each other. Since producers of the show wanted to see relationships develop on camera, they instituted a no-talking policy. Without language, the most integral tool for human interaction, we resorted to communicating with our eyes. I confess that many a conversation was held between contestants with a few telling stares.

On the first day of filming, we met downstairs at 6:00 a.m., completely clueless about the tasks ahead. Armed with a minuscule amount of knowledge about nutrition, a calorie counting book, a low fitness IQ, and a healthy dose of nerves, I tried to prepare myself for the unknown. In full athletic gear I boarded a bus with the other contestants, all ready to start this new phase in our lives. A few minutes into the bus ride, we stopped and got out in order to have our ankles taped. At that moment, I was overcome with fear. Normally a person who likes to know what's coming, take time to process, and then formulate a response, I quickly learned that I would not be afforded that luxury on *The Biggest Loser*.

The bus eventually arrived at a beach, where Alison Sweeney stood to greet us. Unabashedly new to this world, I thought, *Wow! I'm actually here face to face with Alison Sweeney!* I was star-struck. (Just for the record, she is even more beautiful in real life than she appears on the show.) Once we were all out of the bus and excitedly ran onto the sand, Alison informed us that we'd be completing a mile— the last mile of season seven's marathon run. I was immediately so relieved, thinking, *What a great challenge! I can do a mile!* How meaningful to start our journey where the previous season left off. I vividly remember watching Tara cross the finish line in, at the time, record time. I was confident that I could make it to the finish line of this particular contest. Still, as competitive a person as I am, I knew there was no way I could run the entire mile—something I had done only once in my life at the age of twelve. We began in the sand, so I jogged as best as I could to get out of the sand and onto the road. I was already huffing and puffing, so I thought, *I'll power-walk it!* Taking comfort in the knowledge that only a few people were ahead of me and most were behind me, I blocked everyone else out, kept a steady pace, and gave it everything I had.

I walked along and quickly noticed that this was certainly not flat terrain. Hill after hill challenged me to work harder, but I was taken aback by the absolutely gorgeous scenery: the mountains, the ocean, the sand—I could see God in everything. It was wonderful to be out in the sunshine, feeling my blood pump through my body. I had no grand design of winning; I just wanted to do my best. My plan became to walk up the hills and jog back down, but soon enough I was back in the sand. The sand was insanely hard to maneuver in. I was still walking when someone shouted, "Come on, Abby, dig in." On command, I forced my legs to (I'm being generous here) run. Jogging once again, I crossed the finish line in fifth place with a time of just over seventeen minutes. The fastest mile I'd done in recent history was twenty minutes on the treadmill. I felt glorious! I couldn't breathe or move for a solid ten minutes, but I was filled with pride for what I'd been able to do.

Daniel finished first, which I thought was fantastic. All of us were used to coming in last, used to being the slowest.

Daniel came from being the biggest and the slowest the prior season to being the best. He was redefining his story, and I was so happy to see him get that confidence boost. Suddenly, Tracey, another contestant who was suffering from the heat and overexertion, had to be airlifted to the nearest hospital. Then Mo fell ill and had to join her. All of the commotion halted filming, leaving us on the beach for over three hours. We took advantage of our dreamy surroundings and removed our shoes to walk in the ocean. I felt exuberant! The day was beautiful, and the future seemed bright.

When we finally arrived back at the ranch, we began the grueling task of sharing our stories. By that time, it was evening and we'd been up since dawn, completed a mile, and watched two contestants go to the hospital. Add fear and anxiety to the fatigue, and it had certainly been an arduous day. Listening intently, I was struck by Sean's story. He had the most beautiful spirit; I could see the light in him, and I instantly loved him. The next story was Shay's. I'd felt a strong connection with Shay and loved her immediately upon seeing her, but we hadn't yet talked or spent time together. When Shay talked about her past, I cried. She told us how she had a heroin-addicted mother and had grown up in foster care. The pain in her eyes made me feel something for someone other than myself for the first time in two and a half years. It had been so hard for me to feel true empathy for someone else after the wreck, but I felt compassion and pain for Shay. I was experiencing authentic feelings for the first time in a long time.

I told my story last. Many of the contestants were visibly bothered by my words; many cried. When it was time to pick partners, I was emotionally whipped, crying, and embarrassed for crying in front of people I barely knew. At least at that point I wasn't hungry. Allen chose me as his partner, and I was elated to have avoided being picked last.

Thinking we'd certainly be whisked off to bed, I was unpleasantly surprised to hear that we were headed for our first weigh-in. I was instantly uneasy. Mortified, I followed the other contestants to change into a sports bra and spandex—the outfit of champions. For someone at the pinnacle of modesty, I was catapulted out of my comfort zone. I knew my body was not attractive—definitely not something I wanted to show off. I'd always thought my spirit and my insides were attractive, but I had no delusions when it came to my body. Being so exposed, forced to reveal myself in what I called my "naked clothes," was beyond degrading.

When the walls opened to unveil Bob and Jillian, everyone was ecstatic to finally meet them. Jillian warned, "This'll be the last time you're excited about a weigh-in." And I felt like she'd thrown water on the little light I was struggling to hold. She then made a motion like she was cutting off her neck, and I got as far away from her as I possibly could. Skittish by nature, imagine my delight when I saw that my spot for the weigh-in was right next to hers. Here I am standing in *The Biggest Loser* gym with Jillian Michaels right next to me with my name illuminated above the scale. Surreal!

I stepped onto the scale and saw the imposing "247"

appear on the screen. Alison asked, "Well, what do you think of 247?" "It surprises me, but it doesn't define me," I replied. Strongly grounded in the knowledge that I didn't hate myself, the number did not sway me. I didn't like the body I was in, but the weight itself was not the problem. The person on that scale was broken, and that's what I was there to fix. I kept asking myself, *Why are you here?* My objective was to find a purpose in life again and feel like life mattered. After that first weigh-in, we picked roommates, and Shay and I immediately made eye contact, ending that excruciatingly long day on a much-needed positive note. Little did I know just how important that decision would be.

The very next day was our first workout in the gym. Jillian got a hold of Shay and many others right away, launching me into panic mode. At one point I heard Bob Harper say my name, and I thought he was coming for me. The look on my face must have said it all because I remember the camera guy laughing. (The audio and camera crews don't interact much with the contestants because they are there to record what's going on rather than influence our stories.) I walked on the treadmill at an incline for an hour and a half without stopping before Jillian came for me. Now, at this stage in my journey, I can objectively look back and see that Jillian's heart was in the right place. But then, I thought she was mean. As I stepped onto the StairMaster, she informed me, "Your purpose is to climb the stairs." Being the overly sensitive person I am, I took her words as a slap in my face in my quest to find purpose again. I went from scared to mad. I thought, *How dare she belittle me when I can't get any lower.*

Taking me across the gym, Jillian led me through three sets of hop-overs, body weight pull-ups, a mountain crawl across the gym floor, a wall squat (with her standing on top of me), a run on the treadmill without turning it on, and ten pull-ups on the treadmill. I was sweating from every orifice of my body, including my hands. As much as I tried, my own body weight was more than I could handle and I could not hold on to the bar. As I fell to the treadmill more than once, I felt like a complete and utter failure. Instructing me to hold the last one, she partially stood on me and said, "God is not going to get your ass off this treadmill." I decided we weren't going to be friends.

My tender heart could not handle Jillian in the beginning. I was putting all I had into the workouts and feeling like it just wasn't good enough. That night I talked to Shay about Jillian, and she basically told me to figure out a way to deal with it, that Jillian wasn't going to change. Void of any coddling or sugarcoating, Shay's words were just the advice I needed; I appreciated her ability to give sound counsel in a way that was neither nice nor mean, just real. With a renewed mind-set, I knew the only thing that I could control was me. I couldn't simply pity myself and my situation, thinking if only the people around me would change, things would be easier. I turned to the ultimate counselor, God, to pray for a change within my own heart.

Lying alone in bed that night, I cried and prayed fervently for over an hour. Fully aware that people often mirror your feelings about them back to you, I professed that I was not in a good place, and I was going to be dealing with Jillian and interacting with her on a regular basis. I could not function while harboring such negative feelings. I prayed to get to a place where I was at peace, because I refused to let such negativity be my legacy with Jillian. I decided that I wouldn't be scared of her—not that there wouldn't be times when she was very intimidating, but, with God's grace, I chose to focus on the good she was doing. I chose to make our relationship what I wanted it to be. As I've grown to know, Jillian Michaels, despite her tough exterior, has a completely pure heart in her quest to help others. She's an amazing woman, and I am grateful that God put her in my life.

During that first week, we each met with Dr. Huizenga to discuss our specific health issues. I learned that I was at 51 percent body fat with an internal age of fifty-one. As we talked, I told him this time was different. I told him I had changed. Once I decided, truly decided, I was going to get healthy, it was just a matter of time to get the weight off. Needless to say, Dr. H was somewhat skeptical and wanted me to journal what exactly was different this time. I mulled over his question in bed that night.

Today I found out I have 51 percent body fat and my internal age is 51. Oh look…they match…I'm really relieved there's not more wrong with me. Seriously. Like I said before, it's a starting point.

Why have all the other diets failed? Because I had really superficial reasons and misinformation. We have a tendency to listen to what we want to hear. Look at every infomercial on T.V. Quick, easy. If given the choice humans typically will take the easier route. Health reasons sound great, but the real reason I've ever tried to lose weight before was because I wanted other people to like me.

Why is this time different? I like me! Sure I want others to like me, but my worth is not determined by what others think of me. I have zero fear of death, but I still choose life.
—written in May 2009 while on The Biggest Loser *ranch*

For most *Biggest Loser* contestants, death is the persuasive factor; they fear that they'll die if action is not taken to reverse the damage done to their bodies from years—in some cases, a lifetime—of obesity. That is what made me different. In my case, the scary thing was to continue living out my days in the mindless, emotionless, purposeless state in which I'd been living. Some things are worse than death.

The next few days were "dark days," meaning there was no filming. We hiked a mountain, and two yellow butterflies followed me the entire way up. I'd always been drawn to the wonder and beauty of the outdoor world, in awe of the perfect union of nature's elements. Outdoor activities, where I could truly see God's glory made manifest in the natural world, were much more rewarding and enjoyable than being in the gym on the equipment.

I longed for word from home. Removed from everything familiar, my mind wandered to thoughts of what my family might be doing, how my dad's shoulder was healing from the rotator cuff surgery he had undergone just before I left, and how the students and teachers were preparing for the end of the school year. I often spoke into the microphone attached to my chest, "Letters from home, letters from home," in my own little sing-along tune, hoping that the person assigned to transcribe my every word might communicate my desire for letters to the producers. In actuality, although my family and friends began sending letters very early on, they were being held hostage, and I did not receive one letter from home until my seventh week on the ranch. Still, that didn't stop my mother and many others from writing.

My dearest Abby,

Wow, it's been a long time since we've talked. Miss you, as I know you miss many back home. I think of you often, wondering what you are doing, and how! As difficult as I can't imagine it is, my prayer is that you have been able to dig deep as you have had to do, and do those things which seem impossible. "I can do all things . . ."

It's amazing the number of people who inquire if we have heard from you and how you're doing . . . To which I reply, no, but later is better than sooner! . . . and they continue to pray for you.

. . . I heard on the news there was an earthquake near LA, and wondered if you had felt it. Probably not . . . you were probably running so fast, you just thought the earth was moving beneath your feet!

I'm still walking every morning . . . sometimes pushing myself a little more than usual because of my guilt of thinking how hard you must be pushing yourself. I know you must read 1 Cor. 9:25–10:13 and take strength . . .

Abby you are still my hero! And I mean that whether you come home tomorrow or whenever. I believe in you... and as Dad says, "God + you = a majority!"

I look at the stars and moon at night and think Abby is looking at the same ones, and feel connected. We pray for you without ceasing and love you more than life. Stay strong in His strength...

All our love,
Mom and Dad

Other than the complete lack of contact with my family and friends, the production schedule was the hardest part for me. Back at home my routine consisted of driving to work, sitting in a chair, sitting at lunch, sitting on desks, driving home, sitting in my chair, walking to the bathroom, maybe driving through a drive-thru, sitting and making jewelry, or sitting and watching television. I was as inactive as is humanly possible. On the ranch, I was not only more active than I'd ever imagined I could be, I was also on constant alert—waiting for the next twist to be disclosed. I hated not knowing how long workouts would last or if we'd have to go back for more. We didn't know about challenges until we walked out and saw Alison Sweeney. Never knowing what was going to happen next, with multiple cameras readily available to catch every move and every facial expression, my mind was in a perpetual state of upheaval.

The morning of the first last-chance workout, I got out of bed and couldn't walk. A horrible, sharp pain in my knee left me crying in agony. I knew what sore felt like by then, but this was truly hurt. I somehow made my way downstairs to ice it. Bob and Jillian came in to evaluate me, and I knew I'd be fighting an uphill battle. They are both accustomed to people who make up excuses and use injuries as reasons to sit out of workouts. Fortunately, they agreed to put me in the pool for exercise that day, or so I thought. Ten minutes into my pool workout, Daniel delivered a message from Jillian: *Get out of the pool and come to the gym. And hurry!* I limped out of the pool and stepped painfully toward the gym. Inside, I pedaled on the bicycle until Jillian came to work with me. We then worked on boxing moves, arm lifting, and rowing. It was clear to me that she took the issues with my knee seriously; Jillian never treated me as though she thought I was overexaggerating or faking my injury. At one point when lifting weights away from others in the gym, I looked up at her and said, "Jillian, the Lord and I had a long talk. And I decided that I love you."

"Well, that's stupid." She laughed as her face softened slightly.

I responded, "Well, maybe so. But it is what it is."

My leg in fact felt slightly better from the salve of the pool, so I enjoyed being able to participate with the others in the gym for our last-chance workout—my last chance to shed more pounds before facing the oppressive scale, a scale that turned out not to be so oppressive after all. I lost fifteen pounds that first week on the ranch, winning the weigh-in and immunity, solidifying my spot for at least another week.

Since it was clear I'd be staying a while longer, I sat down to write a letter to my parents, quickly refreshing my memory of the code we'd developed before I left. To skirt around pesky confidentiality rules, we devised that the number of lines in the first paragraph of my letters home would reveal the weight I'd lost that week. If a letter read "No real news," it meant I had no weight loss news since my last letter. We coined a phrase to represent every color of the rainbow, so I could communicate the color of my team. If I asked about mowing the grass in a letter, it meant my color was green.

> *Dear Mom & Dad,*
>
> *Well...where to begin? There's not a ton I can say. I think I took over 50,000 steps in my first two days at the ranch. I've also had the chance to hike twice to the mountain. The view is absolutely gorgeous! The cast has turned out to be really nice and supportive. I'm very happy with my roommate as well. I'm struggling with the never-ending schedule and my knees. Please pray specifically for those things now. My left knee has (I'm going to give it my best shot here) bursitis. I continue to try to work through the pain, but at times, it's tough.*
>
> *I miss you guys terribly. I hope the mowing at my house hasn't been too much. How is Dad's shoulder? I know rehab must be really rough. I think about you often. Please tell Daren and the girls "hi" for me and that I love them.*
>
> *I love you!*
> *Abby*

Over the next few days, my knee continuously worsened, but I resolved that if I could physically complete an exercise without falling down, I was going to do it. Dr. H and Sandy Krum, the resident medic, encourager, and caregiver, maintained that I had bursitis—inflammation of bursa sacs in the knee, usually brought on by overuse. They advised me to fight through it. So I ran on the treadmill, turned off so I could push the belt on my own power. I limped around just trying to keep up; every step was a pain. I hated being the "injured one."

In the safety of the room I shared with Shay, I revealed my worries and weaknesses, trusting her implicitly with my stories and secrets. I could talk openly with Shay, who—as a survivor of her own circumstances—understood the need to talk about uncomfortable things. She knew there were no words that were going to fix the situation. Shay had the ability to listen to me and affirm my feelings without feeling the need to "fix" things. She just got me and made me feel like she loved my family without ever knowing them; Shay was my safe haven—the lifeline God provided me in human form. Though we'd been raised on polar opposite ends of the spectrum, we were so close and in tune with each other. My life had been easy up to the point of the wreck, whereas Shay had suffered her entire life. On her own journey to healing, she was a little slower to trust and confide in me, but with time, we formed a bond through shared hardship. In retrospect, I'm sure there were times when I wore Shay out with my inexorable need for a faithful confidant. I claimed it in interviews, assuring production crew members that even if Shay was protesting against having to listen to my ramblings, I still loved her, no matter what. I of course knew that she loved me, but in close quarters such a talkative roommate can quickly become annoying! Nevertheless, Shay remained my reliable sounding board. It was the ideal living arrangement for me, and had I lived with anyone else, I would have been miserable and crazy. I needed her in my life.

Later in the second week on the ranch, Dr. Huizenga took another look at my knee. Sandy, the medic on the show, realized from watching me that it was more serious than he'd originally thought. I was in constant, intense pain. Dr. Huizenga put pressure on my knee and I almost came off the table. Tears flooded my eyes, and he said, "I'm 80 percent sure it's a stress fracture. I've never seen anyone with a stress fracture this early." I was relieved to finally have my injury validated, but now I couldn't go on the hikes anymore. Dr. Huizenga didn't want me on unstable terrain. I now had to use crutches. I couldn't use the bicycle. My workout plan now consisted of swimming alone in the pool. Having never been on crutches in my life, I was exceedingly awkward, trying to maneuver my overweight frame. I was not even able to fix my own plate and carry it to the table. Other contestants had to help me with my laundry and tote my things up the stairs in our dorm. I was completely helpless and dependent on others—a most uncomfortable state for me.

One of the most important and difficult lessons I learned on the ranch is that it's okay to accept help and that God did not want me to go through life alone. In the time leading up to my audition for *The Biggest Loser,* I was hell-bent on being "strong," trying to do everything on my own power. I was the lone wolf. I was "fine." (Shay loves to mock this phrase of mine in her faux Texas accent.) Just a couple of weeks into my journey on *The Biggest Loser*, I was far from fine. In a place where I was supposed to feel empowered and confident in my abilities, I was broken to my lowest form, injured and helpless, fighting the words constantly streaming through my mind and weighing on my shoulders: "You're pathetic. You're weak." I thought, *This is supposed to be the good stuff. How much more of the bad stuff am I going to have to go through to finally get to the good stuff?* Yet again, the circumstances in which I found myself were beyond my control, and, forced to depend on God and those around me, I realized that I could not do it alone. God left me with no other option than to lean on Him at a time when I wanted to be self-sufficient and handle it on my own. I wasn't listening, so He sent His message loud and clear: *No, Abby. You will not be handling it. You cannot do this on your own strength; you're going to have to depend on other people. And that does not make you weak.* I finally understood the true lesson: I need people—even when some people disappoint me, even when some people let me down. My ultimate comfort and joy comes from God, but God put people in my life to help me on my journey. It was time for me to embrace and appreciate that gift.

As part of a pop challenge during the second week on the ranch, we gathered at the Four Seasons hotel to learn cooking tips from Curtis Stone. I spotted a man wearing a "TirePro" T-shirt (the name of the company my brother works with in Texas) and did a double take. Anxious for some taste of home, when he passed by me I said, "My brother is a TirePro dealer in Texas." Surveying my face, he correctly identified me as Daren Day's sister and promised to tell everyone hello for me. In all its randomness and triviality, the encounter was utterly meaningful to me; what a blessing to run across a piece of real life while inundated with the world of reality television—a process that felt strikingly unnatural.

Back home in Mabank, my parents took on not only the daily demands of my life—paying my bills, collecting my mail, keeping up my home—but also communicating and updating my extended family and friends on this new chapter in my life. My mother took to cyberspace to keep my family of supporters, whether lifelong or brand-new, up to speed on any bit of news she could get her hands on. And news traveled quickly.

May I begin by saying as insignificant as I am in the world God created, He loves me a lot and bypassed all the "important" people in Hollywood to comfort my lonely heart...

Daren, Abby's brother, owns a tire store in Mabank and serves on a national tire council with a company named TirePro. Today, Daren gets a call from a bigwig in the company who is at a meeting in Los Angeles at the Four Seasons (apparently with a TirePro sign around). He proceeds to tell him that a young lady came up to him and said, "My brother is a TirePro dealer in Texas." One look

*at her and he said it must be Daren Day, you look just
alike! He said they were filming at the Four Seasons for*
The Biggest Loser *and she looked great and happy and
said to tell everyone hi!*

*I hope this made your day as it made mine! Thanks
for all your continued prayers and I'll keep you posted on
anything I can!*

Billie

—e-mail sent Wednesday, May 27, 2009

My newfound willingness to depend on other people
came in handy sooner than expected as we faced a group
challenge in week two at the ranch. The second week
already brought added pressure with the threat of a double
elimination unless we lost a combined total of 150 pounds.
Now, scanning a series of boards and platforms arranged
over water, we listened as Alison explained the risks and
rewards of this particular challenge. One by one, each
contestant had to balance on the boards and move toward
each platform without falling into the water, until every
person stood on one platform together. If one person fell
into the water, the challenge was over. Progress then continued toward the next platform, as the connecting boards
gradually narrowed. The eventual goal was to occupy the
fourth and final platform, where we'd be rewarded with a
twenty-pound advantage in the weigh-in and a phone call
home. I desperately wanted that phone call. As the challenge began, we teetered and wobbled and swayed but we
made it to the first platform. Encouraging and helping each

other the entire way, we traveled along the boards to each destination, coming to the finish with every contestant and a strong sense of accomplishment in tow. I could not wait to call home and hear my parents' voices!

Okay . . . Abby called tonight!!!! I'm afraid not much to report . . . I think all we did was cry and say I love you! It will all probably sound pretty stupid when it airs.

She did say it was REALLY hard and when we said we prayed without ceasing, she said DON'T STOP! She also said she had climbed a mountain . . . and at the top were two butterflies (which are really significant to her). It was only for 5 minutes, which just flew by. At the end, she said tell everyone hello.

We did get 2 letters from Abby today! She didn't/couldn't say a lot but that the cast was nice and supportive, she liked her roommate, the view is gorgeous, but mostly that her knees are killing her and to pray specifically for that!

The second one said she had been in the pool 5 or 6 hours that day, hoping her knee would feel better after a day of rest. She had finally read the letters we sent with her and they really provided a boost, said she would probably read them once a week! Said she was learning a lot about nutrition, but the kitchen is really crowded so she doesn't get to cook much, but there are some really good cooks who are willing to share . . .

The last line said to tell everyone hi and KEEP PRAYING!

> *Our love to each of you,*
> *Billie*
> —e-mail on Friday, May 29, 2009

The third week on the ranch resulted in Sean's and Antoine's departures and an intensifying bond between Shay, Daniel, Rebecca, Amanda, and me. We'd started having late-night conversations in my room. They let me talk about my family without being uncomfortable. I was able to listen to their stories with empathy and compassion. We never discussed voting or anything about elimination; we just knew we had the loyalty and the true friendships to stay as long as we wanted. I also enjoyed when Julio kept me company in the pool. Those workouts could be so isolating with everyone else in the gym, but he often broke the monotony with a race or his unique perspective on life. I treasured the new relationships I'd found. After the week three weigh-in, tired but proud of my progress, I wrote home in a letter to my parents.

Dear Mom & Dad,

Well, things on The Biggest Loser *ranch are as crazy as ever. "T.V. weeks" don't always match up with real weeks, but we are still going strong. We've met lots of different people and have seen so many different things. I'm adjusting to the schedule better and have cultivated several friendships that I cherish. I remind myself every day that I won't "play" the game. I will stay true to what is right for me.*

It was so good to talk to you on the phone! Hearing your voices brought me much joy! I've been trying to take lots of pictures to give you glimpses at this world . . .

Please continue to pray for my knee, for strength, and wisdom. I like to compare the ranch to the Real World but on steroids. ☺ *Luckily people have been really kind and good to me.*

(Big breath) *Ok, I wasn't going to say anything, but I found out I have a stress fracture in my left knee. I'm getting excellent care, but I need to make sure all my insurance stuff is in line. I saw an orthopedic specialist who was fantastic. I'm on crutches for a couple of weeks and will be spending lots of time in the pool.*

Finishing this off quickly so I can send this today.

Love you!
Abby
P.S. *I* PROMISE *I'm ok.*

Despite my early connections with certain people, those first few weeks when everyone was bonding late at night, staying up, working out, talking, and getting to know each other, I was in bed. I had to sleep or I was crazy. As social as I am, it took everything I had to get up and participate. My body was in shock; my mind was in shock. I'd ice my leg, read a bit, and fall asleep out of pure exhaustion. An upside was going to USC to see a gait specialist who told me why I had a stress fracture of the tibia. He explained that overweight people compensate by not bending when they walk, placing excessive weight and pressure on their joints and weakening their glutes and hamstrings. I needed to strengthen those muscles to absorb the pressure causing my injury.

Dear Mom & Dad,

No real news, just wanted to check in.

I just wanted to clarify about the stress fracture . . . it's actually in my tibia, and it should heal completely. I'm much better on crutches these days. My arms are getting much stronger, too. Several fellow cast members are kind enough to cook for me.

There's so much going on every day. It's wild being on this end of the show. There are hundreds of production, audio, casting, and art department folks. It's crazy to see just how many people it takes to make the show run. There are several people I really appreciate. They go out of their way with kindness and words of encouragement.

I am staying true to my resolve not to play the game. The relationships I've formed are genuine, and I have no "alliances." My only goal when I walk off the ranch is to have my integrity intact . . . so far, so good. Ok . . . off to sleep.

Love you!

Abby

Into the fourth week I was beginning to resign myself to life on crutches. I knew I was doing everything I could— eating cleanly, writing everything down, and swimming constantly. Life on the ranch remained just as hectic and unpredictable, and I remained just as tired and uneasy. The idea that the ranch is equal to a spa vacation couldn't be further from the truth. Contestants make their own food, do their own dishes, and clean out the refrigerator—jostling for space in a tiny kitchen. Unable to help with cooking or cleaning because of my knee, I was assigned the task of making a grocery list. One night, up making a grocery list at 11:00 at night, I barely held my head up as Shay walked in from the gym. She immediately asked, "What are you doing up?" I told her I was making a grocery list. Shay looked at everyone and said, "It's past Abby's bedtime. I'm going to do the list. She has to go to bed; she can't stay up this late." And she sent me to bed. Shay was my protector, allowing me time to process the day, renew my strength, write letters home, and prepare for the next day.

Dear Mom & Dad,

Another busy week here at the ranch. I'm still swimming a ton and feel good about what I'm doing. I would love to be healed completely, but it will come in time.

I wish I could give specifics about all the "happenings" here, but it will be great while we're watching the show to know what really went on behind the scenes. I'm happy to say that nothing about this world is really appealing. I'll enjoy the process and the scenery and return home happily.

Oh, my goodness . . . a couple of weeks ago when we were out and about I saw a guy wearing a TirePro shirt, and he knew Daren. I think his name is Ed. What a small world. Also, another day, some guys on the crew asked if I was Abby and said they knew Travis Poe. (He was best friends with Tal and big in the OAP world.) Crazy indeed.

Kristen said she talked to you today. She assured me that you were okay and not overly worried. I pray that is true. I really am going to be alright, and I'm going to make sure my knee (tibia) is healing properly before I jump back in.

I hope Dad's shoulder is doing tons better. I know the rehab must be grueling.

My roommate is still fabulous! She is solid and down-to-earth, and I am so thankful to know her. You will love her as well. Please pray for her as much as you pray for me.

My letters jump around so much, but I have to write quickly and stop and start several times. All this to say, I have to sleep now.

I Love You!
Abby

P.S. Tell everyone hello for me. Also, I have no idea when/ if we get letters, but I know you can send them in now. Please get letters from my friends, too.

Every single day on the ranch ended in downright exhaustion. We were working out all day, randomly getting pulled to do interviews. Simply walking was painful because of the injury; my leg throbbed constantly. By 11:00 p.m. when the day's events finally ceased, I was spent and wanted nothing more than to crumple into a ball on my bed. Instead, we were required to stand for "morph photos"—taken regularly in front of a green screen to show us progressively shrinking. Normally, I consider myself a smiler—I can put a smile on my face any time, any place; well, not at this time and not in this place. I stood there for my morph photo with my big broad shoulders and big fat T-shirt and was too tired to smile. The first pictures were blown up and posted on the wall in black-and-white.

There we were in all our glory. They were truly the funniest pictures ever. I gave nicknames to the photos, dubbing mine "Whipped Dog" in tribute to my beaten-down look. The last time I could remember feeling so drained was at the start of my job at South Terrebonne. Thinking of my friends in Louisiana, I imagined the laughs we would have had in the lounge over my morph photo.

For the many of you from ST, thank you for opening your hearts and lives to our Abby and showing such great support. I wanted to share this e-mail from a fellow teacher at South Terrebonne HS in Houma. And the picture speaks volumes...

"Team Rike" appears on the headstone at Elm Grove Cemetery, but obviously Team Rike lives on...

Billie

Here is the original message from Madge Gautreaux.

Mrs. Billie,

Thank you so much for the updates on Abby. I'm sure you miss her desperately as we do here at ST. A few of her buddies got together to make "Team Rike" T-shirts and we took a photo. I will mail it to her (understanding that she may not get it). However, I wanted to send you a copy as well. I have attached it to this e-mail.

It is not easy to express the impact Abby had on the people here. When I first met her, I had no idea of the tragedy she endured. But something about Abby made me want to keep her close, and seek her advice and her friendship. After

*she courageously shared her story with me, my heart shat-
tered into a million pieces. She is a truly wonderful, amazing
human being. By the grace of God, Abby has come into my
life. She has opened my eyes in so many aspects, and she has
shown me what true faith is.*

*Kudos to you and your husband for raising such an
amazing woman. There are great things in store for Abby, and
my instincts tell me she will take Hollywood by storm. They
won't know what hit them on* The Biggest Loser.

*I will be praying not only for Abby, but also for God to
continue to fill your heart with peace in knowing that your
baby is safe and happy.*

Madge Gautreaux
—e-mail sent Friday, May 29, 2009

At the beginning of week five, Brandon Roberts, a story
producer, joined us on the ranch, and I was instantly grateful for his approach. He was the first person who would
just observe; he really wanted to get a feel for the dynamic
of the house at a time when things were becoming a little
tense and a real division was beginning to take shape after
we split into two teams. I likened myself to Switzerland and
stayed neutral despite obvious bonds with certain people.
I just wasn't a part of any game playing, not only for personal reasons, but also because I physically could not play
the game. I may have set a record on *The Biggest Loser* for
sitting out the most challenges in the show's history. Every
challenge, while everyone else was sweating and competing and getting small deposits of success, I was standing on

the sidelines "cheering" for everyone else. I felt isolated and separate from the group the majority of the time.

Up to that point, though super nice, no one on the production crew was asking in-depth questions about my family, and when I did talk about them, I could sense growing levels of discomfort. Brandon asked questions unapologetically; he didn't tiptoe around the story. In fact, he shared stories about the loss of his mother and how that impacted him. Sometimes, people who have experienced great loss or have been through traumatic events have an understanding of it. They know that the human spirit is resilient. Brandon wasn't afraid to say the wrong thing, so he asked, "What was it like?" I was so relieved; I desperately wanted to talk about my family. I wanted people to know me, and my family was and is a huge part of me. I couldn't talk about them enough.

As the week continued, the contestants were presented with a challenge that I could finally participate in! The only physical movement required was the spinning of a wheel. However, as I listened to Alison explain that we risked having to eat high-calorie foods with each spin and that the ultimate prizes were money and the power to choose teams and trainers, I was no longer tempted at all. I'd already accepted that God put Jillian in my life and she would be my trainer. It didn't matter. The only thing I could control was me, and I was certainly not going to ruin all my hard work on one fattening cupcake.

When I began my Biggest Loser *journey, I was at a super low point personally and desperately wanted to get some semblance of a life back. I decided before I ever went to the ranch that, though it was technically a game, it wasn't a game for me. My goal was to physically feel better, emotionally heal, and form real bonds with people based on truth and honesty. To some, my view may be a bit naïve . . . I can deal with that. =) (Just for the record, that happened.)*

When we were faced with that temptation, I wasn't all that tempted. My life experiences tell me that regardless of how much we think we control the happenings of our life, we really don't. Furthermore, it didn't matter to me if I trained with Bob or Jillian because they are both wonderful people. It didn't matter to me who was on my team. It did, however, matter to me if I had to eat a 1,000-calorie piece of cake. I was still on crutches, limited to only swimming, and I could not afford one extra calorie. My choice was not a very popular one in that it did not make for good TV . . . I can live with that, too. At the end of the day, we all have to make choices we can live with. Though I am very, very, very far from perfect, I can live with all the choices I made.

—written as a note on Abby's Facebook page as "Why I Didn't Participate in the Week 5 Temptation" on Thursday, October 15, 2009, at 4:33 p.m.

During week six the blue team won a trip home for the week but strategically chose to pass it on to us, the black team. I was thrilled! In a wheelchair at the airport, I was on cloud nine, getting to see my family and have a chance to regroup. I felt like the whole time I'd been at the ranch, they'd been dunking me. I could get up long enough to gasp for air, only to go under again. So for the first time since beginning the journey, I was really getting to catch my breath. Going home to see the people who loved me and missed me was therapeutic and restorative. Recognizing that everyone was fine and that I was in fact doing the right thing sent me back to the ranch with a new resolve.

Sorry about being so long in updating you on Abby's homecoming . . . we just woke up! Seriously, we had an absolutely wonderful, long-awaited, really needed visit . . . with lots of hugs and late-night talks. Abby came in Friday evening, so we had parts of Saturday and early Sunday pretty much for family time . . . the other parts spent in the gym! Then the camera crew was here Sunday afternoon.

She looks absolutely gorgeous . . . thinner, with a California tan! She is on one crutch now, still unable to do much working out other than in the pool. She's quite the Michael Phelps . . . one lap after another. Her injury, which occurred the FIRST week, and diagnosed the second (you know how they think everybody's faking it!) has prevented her from participating in lots of gym activities.

There's so much we can't share . . . in fact, everyone at the party signed a release to use their pictures, and a statement that they would not share the details of the evening or any pictures taken until after the episode had aired . . . under penalty of a $500,000 fine!!! Since we are sharing this with only her most intimate friends, we know that none of you would post anything on Facebook, notify newspapers, or the like! We aren't sharing any pictures because of this!

The party was just great BECAUSE of a lot of wonderful family and friends who made it possible. We can never adequately express our thanks to each of you.

When we took Abby back to the airport Tuesday morning, we thought... it had been one week since the first phone call came that Abby might get to come home; then the 2 am confirmation Friday morning; Abby arriving Friday afternoon at DFW; 46 attending a welcome home barbeque Sunday (that I might add was hotter than !@!@!!... weather, not the barbeque!!!); a camera crew of 4 who didn't leave Sunday evening until after 11; filming at the gym at 9:00 am on Monday; interviews here at the house that afternoon; filming at Two Senoritas in Canton with students at 4:00; back to our house for interviews at 6:30 until after 11 pm; to the airport in Dallas Tuesday at 9:20 am!

Folks this is all waaaaaaaaaaay out of our comfort zone and we have no intentions of moving to Hollywood... and know that Abby can't wait to NOT move to Hollywood. During the three filming episodes here at the house, they rearranged every piece of furniture and all that was on it... guess it's all in the details! But they were all so friendly and nice and put everything back... even the dust! Thank you all for your patience during the filming at the party... we were packed in; had to turn the fans OFF for the filming, and most of all to each of you from Abby: she felt so badly afterwards that she didn't spend enough time with everyone, especially after most of you driving so far and enduring the heat. Hopefully, next time... or sometime soon, it will be longer, and there won't be a camera following her every step.

Speaking of next time! Abby has been gone for 6 weeks, so we are assuming it's about halfway through for a 12 week season (mid September to mid December)... and these are all assumptions! She obviously could be coming home any time, and it will be on about a 24 hour notice! After the elimination, you fly home the next day! Since they have just had a camera crew here, we have no idea if they will send another one, but many of you (especially those from Louisiana who couldn't make this one) have expressed a desire to be here. We will notify everyone of the event and just see what works out... maybe a public venue that holds lots of people!

Thank you again... for loving our Abby... and showing it in so many, many ways! She needs wisdom, endurance, and healing.

Till next time,
r & b
—e-mail written on Wednesday, July 1

After my much-needed week at home, I began to adjust to life as a *Biggest Loser* contestant, and it wasn't so scary. I wrote a letter to my parents saying that I was finally in a better place and ready to stay. I was back to me, getting my snap back. I launched into an unprecedented (at least for me) workout regimen and burned more calories that week than ever before. I was down to one crutch and running on an AlterG treadmill, which I affectionately called my "bubble machine." It lifted half of my body weight, allowing me to run at one hundred pounds instead of two hundred. I felt fantastic, comfortable in my surroundings, finally getting my bearings. Having burned enough calories to lose seven or eight pounds, it never crossed my mind that I might be going home.

Any homesick feelings I'd had were assuaged not only by my recent trip back, but also by the show's decision to finally deliver the letters from family and friends that they'd been holding on to all this time, even ones my parents had written after my phone call home in week two. I was finally able to read the words of hope and encouragement, the prayers sent by dozens of people. Their positive energy made me even more dedicated to completing the task I'd set before myself seven weeks earlier.

> *My dearest Abby,*
>
> *Wow! 5 minutes is really quick!*
>
> *When Kristen called and said you had won a challenge and your prize was a call home; well, needless to say, we were ecstatic. She said you were "kicking butt" and hadn't fallen below the yellow line, which also thrilled us . . .*
>
> *We received 2 letters from you on Friday, so we went from zero to a hundred, too! Just not like you have! Can't imagine how difficult it must all be. I'm very curious about your schedule if that's not divulging a secret. Also, what you eat. I've stayed "on the wagon" so far, and have missed very few days walking. I feel a lot better . . .*
>
> *Papa spent all morning in here typing a "left-handed" letter to you!*
>
> *Well, my dear, we miss you terribly; but we are so proud . . . that you dare greatly, pick yourself by the scruff of*

*the neck, and do what has to be done! You are amazing and
you are my hero! (And if you come home next week, not one
feeling will change!) God has seen you through the worst of
times and He will see you through these. He is the same,
yesterday, today, and tomorrow . . . thank goodness something
doesn't change!*

I love you. I love you. I love you.
Win another challenge so we can talk again soon . . .

Love and prayers without ceasing,
I love you, Mom
Let us know if we can send you anything!

*Boy was it great to hear your voice last night. You sounded
great. We can't tell you how much we have missed you. You
are a breath of fresh air. I truly hope things are going good for
you. We were absolutely thrilled you won the challenge to get
to call home . . .*

*I assure you that you have been prayed for, continuously
without ceasing. Especially at night, I pray for you to have
renewed strength, endurance, and stamina . . . My prayer for
you also has been for you to be in the center of God's will that
He might use you in a special way to gird you up, strengthen
you, love you, and speak through you. I've told Mom how
much I admire and respect you because you are a strong person
who sees right and wrong and you stand up for right, even if
it means sticking your neck out. But you are able to do it not
only with your heart, but with your intellect and your ability to*

*communicate what needs to be said for right. You have an innate
ability to convey that you care. I never had the intellect, but you
have it, and the personality to achieve your objectives...*

*You can't imagine the people that are praying for you.
We get e-mails daily saying they are praying for you.
Some have expressed what a difference you have made in
their lives...*

*You, Abby, are a very special young lady. I truly believe
God has a big plan for you... The most important thing is
I love you and you know you are very special to Mom, me,
Daren, Madelyn, Maryl, and to all the lives you have already
touched and those you are going to touch.*

God + 1 = a majority

I love you,
Dad

Dear Abby,

*I am so excited to get to write you! Your mom's e-mails
brighten my day.*

*I have probably done more research into BL than anyone
ever. In fact, my computer froze, thus I had to purchase a new
one to remain informed. Jessica Cozart came and set up my
new one.*

*I just pray and pray for you daily for God to hold you
tight and give you strength then I add... and let you win! No
doubt you are competing with everything you've got.*

Blessings, prayers, and love,
Evelyn

Hey Abby Girl,
    *Sad to think you had to get on TV for me to tell you
what an inspiration you are. But, I will also tell you that your
"stardom" is not what inspires. Watching you grow into a loving
person with a passion, that certainly out shines any "stardom,"
for kids that you have taught and the personal giving of yourself to others is what has made me the most proud. Your spirit
of determination and the trials that you have endured allow
others such as myself to hold on to a better understanding of
God's plan for each of us.*
    *No matter the outcome of this event in your life, I know
that someone, somewhere you encountered has been lifted.*
    *You know we all have been praying for your well-being
and safe return and will continue to do so. Personally, I have
never uttered a prayer of you winning, because that has already
been proven.*
    *Keep up the good work, and I must admit I am a bit
anxious to see the new look!!*

Love you bunches,
Uncle Bob

Things with Jillian were greatly improved; she'd even
complimented me during a workout, so unexpectedly that
it momentarily broke my concentration. I enjoyed the praise
but enjoyed the strength I pulled from myself more.

*Jill was nice in the gym. It was a little weird for me. She told
someone that I was as strong as an ox; I just had a bad knee.
Then told me my push-ups were perfect and then something*

else later about doing well. I'm glad she was nice, but the best part is, I didn't need it.
—*written in* Biggest Loser *journal, July 2009*

The night before the weigh-in, Shay was sick and on antibiotics but still set her alarm to wake and work out. I told her NO, that she'd done everything she possibly could, and I was going to take care of it. I knew she would have told me the same had the roles been reversed. Leaving Shay to rest and recover, I set off for the gym at 11:30 at night—totally out of character for me as I was usually in bed. I ran on the AlterG treadmill for an hour and a half until 1:00 a.m. to make sure that I'd get immunity. I did everything I could to guarantee a spot for myself and my teammates for another week.

When I'd first arrived at the ranch, deep down I thought I was going to be the one it didn't work for. I honestly didn't think I could lose weight. I didn't pack smaller-sized clothing to wear once I'd lost weight. Everything in my suitcase was loose and big and comfortable with the exception of one pair of size ten "goal" jeans, required by production. I had more than one good giggle over the seemingly insane thought that I'd ever fit into them. At the time I bought them, I could barely get them past my knees. (I fit into those jeans during the filming of my "Where Are They Now?" segment and gave them away before finale because I could put them on without unbuttoning them.) My mind could not comprehend my body losing weight. I'd always been the type to read the back of the book, unable to stand not knowing the end. Here I was going by blind faith, not knowing my end, having to trust that the process would work for me, and shatter the self-truth I held so dear—that I'd always be fat.

Then everything that could go wrong, did go wrong. At the weigh-in we were matched up with members of the blue team; my competitor was Tracey. I lost the matchup, losing only three pounds. *Three pounds?!* I was shocked. And it just got uglier as we kept losing matchups until it was clear that we'd have to eliminate someone. Assuming that Danny wouldn't win immunity after back-to-back double-digit weight losses, we were floored when he once again lost over ten pounds. As soon as Shay didn't lose enough for immunity, I knew I was going home.

We had to deliberate in our "naked clothes," and I quickly informed my team of my decision. I didn't tell them to vote me off because I was ready to go home; in fact, I'd finally gotten to where I was ready to stay. But I would never vote Shay off, and Daniel and Amanda had really emotional weeks; they needed the experience of the ranch more than I. It was a sacrifice, but I didn't do it so someone could say, "Oh, Abby, great job—you sacrificed!" I knew I'd probably look like a quitter and catch more grief from it than anything. I plainly said, "I'm not fat because I put people first. That is not my story; that is not my truth. The fact is I'm fat because eating is just what I did. It's how I dealt with things. But now I've learned a new set of skills, and I'm putting them into practice. I'll be fine." I realized that sometimes we as humans need to take our own feelings and emotions out of a situation, look at it objectively, and do the right thing.

In the world, we've been sold a terrible bill of goods saying that we need to look out for number one. *It is all about you. You get yours. You need to put yourself first. Do what's good for you and to hell with everyone else.* And that is the reason our society is in the state it is today. Because if no one is ever willing to sacrifice and put someone else first, very little will ever be accomplished! That is part of the beauty that comes from living such devastation; I have a very clear lens that allows me to see the bigger picture. I think that loving yourself is crucial to succeeding in life, but loving yourself doesn't mean you always push yourself to the head of the line. When you truly love yourself, then you're strong enough to let someone go ahead of you and feel good about it.

Leaving the ranch after what turned out to be a very emotional elimination, I did one last interview and listened to my team yell, "We love you, Abby!" from across the yard. I was content, knowing that it was my time and grateful to be leaving at a point when I was ready to tackle the challenge before me.

I'd spoken extensively on the ranch about losing what I called my "heart weight." The physical weight I'd carried to the ranch was a result of poor food choices and a body that had been beaten down by the happenings of life, but it didn't represent who I wanted to and knew I could be. The beauty of my journey was learning to heal from the inside out. I had to learn to need people again, to love people again before that heart weight would lessen. I had to find a purpose within myself once again. It was only when my heart began to heal that my body inevitably followed.

It is the time we have all anticipated . . . Abby has been eliminated tonight and will be home Sunday or Monday! We have to believe that the time is right and we have total confidence that she will do great at home. They want to have a "24 hours later" episode, which is another homecoming! They realize that we just had one two weeks ago, but Brandon will be coming with her and wants another one!

He has given us the option of Sunday or Monday. As usual, it's short notice: Please let us know if you can come and which day would be best for you.

Happy and sad,
r & b
—e-mail written Friday, July 10

CHAPTER 12

The New Me

I learned that courage was not the absence of fear, but the
triumph over it. The brave man is not he who does not feel
afraid, but he who conquers that fear.

—*Nelson Mandela*

Back in Mabank in the middle of July, I decided not to
go back to work the following semester. I wanted to
work on developing the whole me, not just the fitness
me, and to savor this once-in-a-lifetime journey. Still, I was
drained and trying to adjust to going from nonstop action
to nothing. There's definitely an adjustment period when
you come home from the ranch. I still struggled with my
leg and was bored with exercising in the pool. I stayed on
point diet-wise but took about three days off from working
out. Soon I found a walking track in Mabank and started
using it right away. I saw butterflies often along the walking
trail. Being outside and having sun and pretty blue skies and
wind and trees and butterflies fed my soul. Even though I
was by myself a lot of the time, I didn't feel alone. I often

thought about how Rick hated to sweat, and I would giggle. Some days, I ran and thought, *They're cheering me on.* I felt hopeful again. Seeing all the butterflies, I wondered if it was the season for butterflies. I smiled and thought to myself, *Yes. Yes it is.*

It's as GREAT as we anticipated: Having Abby home puts life back into our home that's missing when one of our family is not here! Her homecoming was great as well. She arrived to a crowd of about 100 with a 4-car police escort—4 times! Remember it's Hollywood and the first one might not be just right. When we changed our chant from Abby to Susie they let her out of the car . . . not really . . . But it was fun.

 She looked incredibly gorgeous in a hot pink sleeveless sheath dress and at least 4-inch platform heels! Not sure how good they were on her fracture, but whatever the price . . .

 We have our regulars who are always "there" for Abby, but there were a few surprises as well; and she said it was "absolutely perfect!" Yeah!!! We will always be indebted to the many of you who have been "there" several times for different events for Abby . . . and always with the best hearts! Never complaining that it's too hot, or it's just been two weeks, but always . . . let us know the next time and we'll be there! Attitude makes all the difference!

 Obviously, there are so many people that Abby wants to see and talk to, and she will . . . eventually. She is very committed to this journey until the finale in December. Not sure of all the locations she may train; lotta people and places that want to help her.

We will try to update you if and when there is anything to report; but in the meantime, from the bottom of our hearts, THANK YOU from us and Abby!

r & b

—e-mail written Wednesday, July 15, 2009

Being at the ranch helped me to realize that I was stronger than I knew. I'd gone from having zero energy to wanting to get out of bed and do something. Making a very public commitment gave me built-in purpose; I had reason to get up and work out. I finally had enough knowledge about what foods and how many calories to eat and how to work out. I liked the positive changes in my body; I was now about two hundred pounds in the gym thinking I was hot stuff. I normally wouldn't have thought it possible to lose weight with an injury, but finding the Landry Center introduced me to a whole new way of thinking.

Hello, dear friends and supporters of Abby!

The weeks have pretty much flown by, but with more blessings than we feel we deserve: many of them your continued support and prayers!

Another answer to our prayers and greater blessing than anticipated: The Tom Landry Center in Dallas is providing Abby a place to work out and a personal trainer! This facility is state-of-the-art in every aspect, and they could not have been nicer and more supportive. The trainer is to call her today to set up a schedule (pray that they will be a good match!). She worked out there Friday and Saturday; and we'll go up today. It's about an hour to drive, so it won't be possible to go twice a day, but she will probably go 4 times a week and then swim at the Cain Center in Athens some.

Her knee is healing and she's able to walk some on the treadmill . . . oh yeah, the Landry Center has an underwater treadmill! She has the eating part down to a science, and Whole Foods in Dallas is a great place to find the foods she is used to eating! (We keep telling her that those preservatives and pesticides are really good for us!) Organic and natural— lots of fish, fruits, vegetables, chicken—just commonsense good diet! She made us a fabulous omelet yesterday—(one egg + extra egg white!), asparagus, mushrooms, onions, cherry tomatoes, low-fat cheese, with avocado garnish, turkey bacon, ezekial toast—yummy!

Thank you all again for everything!

r & b

The Landry Center in Dallas is very rehab oriented, subscribing to the philosophy that you can continue losing weight without further injuring yourself. It was the perfect place for me. My only requests when being matched with a trainer were that it be someone knowledgeable and good, but with a kind spirit. My match was Jeremy Allen, a six-foot-two African American man who once played professional football. Nervous and scared, I confessed to him that I'd spent a lot of time in the pool and I lacked confidence in my abilities in the gym. I wanted to start with something that would boost my self-esteem instead of dash it.

Feeling uneasy in a gym setting is not uncommon.

What overweight person actually wants to join an exercise class to fumble through an unfamiliar routine next to Little Miss Skinny and Mr. Muscles? It's like being trapped in a cruel version of "One of These Things Doesn't Belong." The hard truth is that overweight people *do* belong for the mere fact that they are overweight. So often, those struggling with weight tell themselves, "I'll get a trainer or attend a class when I'm more fit." It's like saying you'll go back to church when you stop sinning. In reality, when you're weak, you need other people. When you are out of shape and feel overwhelmed, you need other people.

Starting something new comes with great vulnerability, but one perceived stare or one mean-spirited comment cannot keep you from your ultimate goal. It's my experience that most people in a gym are not nearly as concerned with you as you think. They are too caught up in their own little worlds or they are too worried about what other people are thinking about them to worry about you! Regardless of body shape, everyone has insecurities. Even the most physically fit, beautiful people have issues. When you're an overweight, unhealthy person, you think, *Wow. Look at her. I bet her life is perfect.* I learned long ago that perfection does not exist, and what freedom was in that lesson! Since perfection doesn't exist, I no longer have to waste energy striving for something unattainable. I had to learn to just be me, give it my all, and rejoice in my small victories, knowing that I was creating the change I wanted to see in my life.

Jeremy was a serious, tough trainer, but very kind and never made me feel stupid. He grew to respect my work ethic, and we built a wonderful rapport and friendship. He would push me to the limit, but I could do it! I lifted weights to the point of muscle exhaustion, and if he had to help me on the very last one, he would—just to make sure I completed it. Soon, I had enough confidence to try whatever he wanted me to do. He knew I would give it 100 percent. When my mother came to watch one day, he took straps and put them around him, then around my waist. I power-walked him across the gym floor, warranting stares of disbelief from other men in the gym. Their faces asked, "What is he doing to that poor girl?" I looked forward to working out with him; I was elated to go to the gym and felt stronger than I'd ever felt in my life.

I worked out for about three hours a day and ate right. I was very diligent with my food, but I admit that I was hungry a lot. When I reached my calorie limit, bags of steamed broccoli in the evenings got me through to the next day. Still, I wasn't seeing movement on the scale. I was so discouraged but finally put my faith in what I was doing, trusting that it would work in due time. Weighing 201 pounds at my elimination from the ranch, my body did not want to break the 200-pound plane. It did everything it could to hang on for dear life. Eating 1,200 calories a day and walking at least ten miles a day wasn't doing the trick. It was over two weeks before I saw progress on the scale, but eventually I broke under 200. By that time, I believed in it, and I knew that physically, even at 200 pounds, I felt a lot better than I had at 247. I felt so lucky to have such an amazing opportunity, and I was going to finish what I'd started.

After a few weeks back home in Texas, I returned to Houma, Louisiana, and Vicky Vilcan reached out to me. She got my number from my gym in Louisiana, the Workout Company, and called to invite me to coffee. My mother and I met her at Starbucks where we talked for over an hour. She was so kind and offered for me to work out with her and her trainer Marc Danos when I stayed in Louisiana. Vicky and I began working out together and developed a natural friendship. It was great to have someone who'd been through the same experience and pressure and come out victorious on the other side. Despite public perception, Vicky is loyal, kind, fun, and probably one of the best *Biggest Loser* success stories ever.

Vicky convinced me to attend my first Body Combat class, and I fell in love. It was such a great way to release aggression! The atmosphere of an exercise class also gave me the opportunity to meet new people. I found people like John and Ashley, Emily, Tammy, Anidas, Jen, Crystal, Jason and Tahita, Tami, Jeanie, and a host of other people who shared in my new lifestyle. I had the community for which I longed. What more could I ask for?

I was driving home from the gym the other day and saw a woman walking down the street. Her face and body looked worn and stressed from the trials of life. My heart broke when I saw her eyes . . . they had no life in them. I recognized those eyes . . . As I was driving along I thought of how blessed I was to be in an air-conditioned car with my favorite tunes playing, tired but happy from a great workout, and I thought, Why

Me???? *Why am I blessed to have SO many wonderful people in my life? Why me to have such incredible parents, brother, nieces, cousins, aunts? Why me to have so many people praying for me and supporting me? Why do I get to work out at the Landry Center with Jeremy? Why do I get to do pilates classes with Marie? Why does Vicky share her trainer with me? Why do I have such love and support from people I don't even know? I may never know the why's of this life, but I do know God's grace, and for that, I am thankful!*

—*written as a note on Abby's Facebook page as "Why Me?" on Tuesday, August 18, 2009, at 4:16 p.m.*

As lonely as I'd felt in those years after the wreck, people were now seeking me out instead of avoiding me. I soon looked forward to classes and grabbing coffee afterward. It was very important to me to maintain a balance between "Fitness Abby" and "Social Abby." My story was now much easier for people to handle, since I had so many positive things going on. I'd felt so alone for so long, but now I was able to cultivate new friendships and finally had a place to fit. I met people whom I could share the ugly parts with, who didn't run away. I had a social life again! Finding a balance meant that I was going to work hard and eat right, but that didn't mean I couldn't go out to eat, or go to the French Quarter, or go on shopping trips. I decided to go out and do those things, but pack food or order things really specifically. I made it work for me. I went on *The Biggest Loser* to get my life back, not to sit home alone counting calories.

My biggest victories came not from the scale but from completing workouts with Jeremy and Marc feeling strong. I'd never felt physically strong. I still had days when I was so sore I didn't think I could walk, but I'd go out and walk five miles. I was building confidence in myself, proving to myself that I could do it.

In August, *The Biggest Loser* held an off-camera boot camp at the ranch, offering medical testing, additional nutrition information, and a chance to reconnect with other contestants without the pressure of playing the game. We met in California and set out on a ten- or twelve-mile hike—all downhill. I was used to knocking out over ten miles a day, so I felt strong and capable. We ended up at the ocean, steps away from where we'd completed our very first challenge. Rebecca, Daniel, and I waited at the water's edge for Shay to join us and relished the moment. When Shay arrived, I laid my head on her shoulder and hugged her. Surrounded by breathtaking scenery and buzzing from mood-boosting endorphins, we brazenly stripped down to our Enelle bras (the one I had been photographed in) and spandex and frolicked in the ocean. It was a dreamy day in a picturesque setting with people I loved. I was so thankful.

When the show aired, Facebook became a tool for me to enjoy others' affirmation and praise as they connected with me and sent love and thanks to me for sharing my story.

Well, our first episode is over and think we all agree: God's hands are quite capable!! Two words best describe not only the show but the response: Amazing and Overwhelming.

Abby is amazing (we've known probably longer than most!); but having experienced it ALL with her, and know that her response is: "amazing grace!" We've heard her say more than once: "Don't put me on a pedestal; but if you do, don't make it very high so I won't hurt my head when I fall off!" A real person, with real hurts, experiencing the love of a real God . . . And, then there's overwhelming: the response far exceeds what any of us desired or imagined!

If you aren't on Facebook, get your kids to set you up a page! Abby accepts everyone as a friend (you'll understand the lingo once you get hooked!), but the "amazing and overwhelming" comes on the page set up by Abby's cousin Carley: Google "Abby Rike facebook" and it, along with lots of other stuff, comes up. The posts are OVERWHELMING. People from Guam to Mabank have been touched. And we weep as we read them, praying that God will become as real to them as He is to our Abby.

Wanted to share just one that was posted by Chelsie Bourg, the sister of a student Abby had last year when she taught in Houma. She only had this student from January to April.

"You are far more inspirational than I think you even realize. I truly believe that your dream to make a difference, not only in your life, but to others is happening and will continue to happen. I've seen the light you've brought into my sister's life, and through your testimony, and, well, I can already see the change in my life. Sometimes we can't change the world in the snap of a finger, but just by changing one little thing in someone's heart changes the world for that person. And when we change the world for one person, the domino effect begins. And Abby, you are the root of a flame that will soon have the world on fire. I have no doubt about it. Thank you for making a gift of yourself to the people you know and love, and to the people who are watching you on T.V. God has SO much in store for you. He's never finished with us. And to think, as far as you've come... GREATER things are STILL to be done... GREATER things are yet to come."

> *Thank you all again, and still, for your continuing prayers . . . the journey continues!*
> *r&b*

P.S. Our trip to Houma was quick, but we were thrilled to spend it with Abby and lots of her friends at a "red carpet" party at Shelly and Dave's, many wearing our Team Rike shirts!

The words of encouragement and the prayers were overwhelming and so good for me. My inbox was flooded with over three thousand messages within a few days. The sheer volume of the response was unexpected and unimaginable. Knowing that I could not possibly respond personally to each note, I hoped and prayed that each person would understand how meaningful their support was to me.

Sometimes God is so good it overwhelms me . . . Today as I sat at Starbucks in my sweaty workout clothes, I saw a pretty

*woman walk in with a killer outfit. As she walked past, I
told her she looked great. A few minutes later, she came by
and asked me if I was on* The Biggest Loser. *I thought she
worked out at the Workout Co., but no, she just recognized
me from T.V. (She's the first.) We talked for just a few minutes and she left. She came back a few minutes later because
she had forgotten to get her husband's breakfast. She came back
over to my table and told me that her mother and sister had
been killed by a drunk driver eleven years prior. She told me
my story had touched her, but her story touched me, too. Here
was this beautiful woman thriving after having suffered such
a tremendous loss. We talked about the first years . . . She had
a similar grieving experience with the first and second years
being so long and so short all at the same time.*

—written September 2009

Soon, it was late September and then October, when
anniversary dates appear on the calendar, and I don't do
so well. I e-mailed Jillian and explained that I was having a hard time, to which she responded that I should take
two or three days off. *Wait. Did Jillian Michaels just tell me to
take some time off?* I promptly listened and took two days off
from the gym.

*You have all been the bedrock of Abby's support . . . and we
continue to look to you for that support! This fall has been
and will be wild, and we are thankful to have joyful occasions
in which to look forward. We also have some things we still
grieve over; and that's our request to you: please pray for our*

Abby tomorrow, which would have been our Caleb's 3rd birthday.

As we marveled at how Abby managed to study and earn her master's last fall, we continue to marvel that she is doing what she's having to do to complete this phase of her journey on TBL. It certainly takes all the strength she can muster. Our prayer is for her determination, energy, and strength.

As we think back, we believe that God engineers all circumstances (we're not saying everything is His will, but that He knows everything and it CAN BE used for His will!)... and that He can be glorified in joy as He was in grief.

"...weeping may remain for a night; but joy comes in the morning" (Ps. 30:5). Pray with us that Abby's morning has come...

Our love and thanks,

r&b

—e-mail written Thursday, September 24, 2009

Shortly after, NBC publicist Jill Carmen, an amazing, family-oriented, supportive woman whom I love, called to tell me that *Life & Style* magazine was interested in doing a photo shoot with me. *Me? Really?* They planned to fly me, along with my trainer, to New York. I was down eighty-two pounds at that point and wore a size ten, so I happily sent off my size, then flew off with Jeremy, one of my trainers, to New York—the city where I once honeymooned with Rick.

On location in an incredibly warm, inviting loft with floor-to-ceiling windows overlooking the Hudson, I marveled at the architecture of nearby buildings and the Statue of Liberty in the distance. After hair and makeup, I slipped into the beautiful dresses set out for me to wear. Everyone there was so kind and patient with me; they never became frustrated at my lack of modeling experience. Stepping into a kitchen area, I was joined by a writer and by Kevin Dickson, *Life & Style* Features director. As they began to probe into my story, I was struck by Kevin's compassion and beautiful spirit. He inquired about my faith, wondering how I could possibly believe in a God who had allowed this hideous, horrible thing to occur. As a person who does not share my spiritual beliefs, he was so respectful and willing to not only listen to my story but really hear it. It was unusual for him to hear someone who had a master's degree and spoke intellectually about God with such childlike faith. Kevin did not convey a sense that I was a simpleton or dumb for believing. With no judgment or ridicule, he asked questions from a place of honest curiosity and intrigue. It was the best day I'd had since the wreck. After reading the published article, I was moved by their accurate and heartfelt portrayal of my story.

Walking the streets of New York afterward, Jeremy reported that a woman recognized me as she walked past. Sure enough, the woman came running back with her daughter. She excitedly asked, "Are you Abby from *The Biggest Loser?*" to which I replied, "Yes, ma'am." She surprised me by saying, "Oh, my gosh! We just saw Hillary Duff and now we see you!" As I continued down the street in a fog over being recognized, Jeremy asked, "Do you realize she just put you in the same category as Hillary Duff?" I burst into laughter, thinking, *This is hilarious! Hillary Duff would be so mad!*

What an AMAZING time I had in NYC! I got to shoot the cover of a magazine. ME!!! The cover!

Jeremy, my trainer, and I flew in on Tuesday. A car picked us up at the airport and took us to the hotel in downtown. The Hudson was fabulous! The rooms are small, but very nice. We went to eat, worked out, then watched the show... The next morning Jeremy and I took a taxi to the shoot. (I later learned there was a driver... oops.) I just didn't want to be late. The studio we went to was in the Meat Packing district. It was absolutely one of the most beautiful places I've ever seen. It's just the kind of space I would want. It was old and flawed with tons of character. The windows were from floor-to-ceiling and overlooked the city as well as the Hudson River. The hardwood floors gave such a cozy feel. Then there was the eclectic collection of artwork adorning the walls. FABULOUS! Of course the 20-foot ceilings added to the whole feel of the place. I was ready to move in. Think I will add having a place in NY to my list of dreams. Why not?

We arrived about thirty minutes early. We visited with some of the folks—very relaxed, good vibe. The photographer and lighting folks set up all their equipment. The makeup artist arrived, and around 10 am I began getting made up... As she began straightening my hair, the reporter began asking me questions about diet and exercise tips... After my hair was finished, I did an Access Hollywood *interview. They were so nice, too! The interview went really well... Then it was time to start the photo shoot. Standing in a gorgeous blue dress, on a light blue backdrop, I posed for a cover shot. They put a wind machine (read fan) on me even. I had no clue*

*what I was doing, but they were so patient and nice to me. I
changed dresses a few more times and took similar photos . . .
I'm so happy right now. I LOVE traveling around and
meeting new people. It's exciting! It's fun!
. . . How excited Macy would have been to see her mom
all dolled up! She would have loved to hang out with me
now . . . even more. Now that I have more energy and could run
around. How I wish I had been fit back then. Rick deserved a
beautiful wife. He thought I was beautiful then, I can't imagine
what he would think now. Caleb would be at such a fun age.
How Rick would have loved taking him to UT games!
Recently I have felt almost guilty for being this happy. I
love being a part of something so fun. Of course I would trade
all of this to go back even for a day, but I don't get that option.
I really do want to travel all around and meet new people . . . I
would LOVE to throw myself into work and stay super busy
jet-setting around. It may get old at some point, but right now
it's exactly what I want to do.*
                        —*written in Abby's journal on October 22, 2009*

Home safe and sound the next week, I faced the upcoming third anniversary of the wreck. As each date passes,
whether a birthday or wedding anniversary, I am reminded
that the pain will never leave me. Finding the strength to
focus on working out was almost more than I could handle.

*I had the most unnerving fear after the accident that people
would forget and stop praying . . . thank you for never stopping!
The prayers of those who love us, and of many who don't even*

know us, have sustained us. Can you imagine that it has been three years? As C.S. Lewis put it: "You get over having your appendix out, but when you've lost your leg, you limp the rest of your life." Our limping is propped up by your unending prayers.

And six years ago when Abby and Macy married Rick, Jeremiah 29:11 was printed on their invitation: "For I know the plans I have for you . . . to give you hope and a future." We believe today in that same God who brought them such happiness. We cherish the memories of Rick and Macy and Caleb . . . but we honor them by living, with Abby as our model.

Thank you,
Ron and Billie
—e-mail written Monday, October 12, 2009

Two weeks later, preparing to return to New York to film the *Today Show*, I received notice that I was scheduled to appear on *Ellen* in Los Angeles! Eager to see Shay while in the area, I quickly flew out with my friend Kristin Rose and met up with Shay to hike Runyon Canyon. Kristin has always been fit; she's very tall, lean, and a runner. Why her healthy lifestyle never rubbed off on me before, I'll never know. Hiking Runyon Canyon with her and Shay on a beautiful day in the perfect temperature, I reveled in my two worlds colliding. Two women who'd been with me through very different but equally dark times in my life were now together, bringing my journey full circle. At the very top, I felt like a small child on the oversized bench overlooking the lights of LA as the sun set. The brilliant colors reflected Macy's hair color—a gorgeous orange glow ablaze in the sky. The three of us got to see Macy for a moment in the glorious beauty of the sunset before sitting still to gaze at the twinkle lights stretching out to the horizon. I took it all in: the people I loved, the feeling of hope, the majestic splendor. I was once again so thankful for the moment and for God's never-ending grace. Who would have thought that I'd go from sitting alone at home, slowly fading into the background of my own life, to sitting on a mountaintop, embarking on a whole new adventure? The journey was something I never dreamed possible, and I wanted to drink it in.

The next day I met Ellen DeGeneres. If you think she is warm and genuine on television, she is even more so in person. Due to her unfortunate back injury, hugging Ellen was out of the question, but I felt as though she was sending me love beams the entire interview. It was unreal to be sitting in the chair, visiting with Ellen. During a commercial break, she thanked me for coming and told me she and Portia had watched my elimination episode and then called that night to see about having me on the show. I shared with her how much Macy loved her. I explained, "Macy loved Dory. We were a big Nemo family. Macy quoted you and danced around singing to you on many occasions. So I have to tell you that you provided immeasurable joy for my family. When I was in the pool at *The Biggest Loser* ranch, my mantra the whole time was 'Just Keep Swimming.' I must've said it a thousand times in my head." Shortly after our brief exchange, I was ushered offstage and left to catch the red-eye flight to New York to meet my mother, flying from Dallas to join me for the *Today Show*.

Arriving in New York, I freshened up a bit at the hotel room with my mother, and, after a much-needed sugar-free Red Bull, headed to the NBC studio. What a whirlwind it all was! After hair and makeup, I did a quick interview and walked out to crowds of people who'd gathered to watch. Cheers erupted and people yelled, "It's Abby! It's Abby!" bringing my mother to tears.

Deciding to stay an extra three or four days in New York, Mother and I were like true New Yorkers walking to Central Park. We have been known to shop a little, so we couldn't pass up a boutique with French couture dresses. I needed a finale dress, right? As I browsed, my mother proudly told the saleswoman about my stint on *The Biggest Loser*, inciting the saleswoman to share a story of her own. She didn't watch the show but did buy *Life & Style* magazine. She said, "I read your story, then laid hands on your picture, made the sign of the cross, and prayed over you. Now God has brought you to my store." What an amazing moment!

We never would have had such a memorable time in New York had we not both been fit. My mother was down fifty or sixty pounds by then. The act of walking never occurs to an overweight person, especially one from a small town where driving is paramount and walking is not part of the culture. Walking several miles to Central Park that day and several more miles within Central Park, my mother and I were able to experience New York in a whole new way; we didn't even know what we'd been missing. I can't put a price on that experience with my mother.

Back home at the end of November, with Macy's birthday and *The Biggest Loser* finale right around the corner, I was shaken out of my temporary haze by a phone call about going on the Jay Leno show to perform a weird talent—in my case, making strange animal noises. I flew out to film right before Thanksgiving and met fellow *Biggest Loser* cast members Filipe, Sione, and Roger. So nervous, embarrassed, and giggly, I walked out, met Jay Leno, then performed my dramatic interpretation of a dolphin and a group of pigs. That three minutes of glory, no matter how awkward, was just the medicine I needed to make it through the holiday.

Shay was able to come in the dressing room with us and hang out before I once again caught the red-eye back to Dallas to run the 5K Turkey Trot on Thanksgiving Day with my brother. I arrived home, changed clothes, and ran the race. Later, we attended a Dallas Cowboys game and ended up in a suite. As the chaos of the past few weeks came to an end, I was ready for finale and the end of my weight-loss journey.

If you hear funny animal noises coming from your TV during the Jay Leno *show Wednesday night . . . it will be Abby! She will catch the "red-eye" Wednesday after the show and arrive Thanksgiving around 6:00 a.m. . . . so she can get to White Rock Lake for the 5K Turkey Trot!! Daren*

and Ron and I will meet her up there and have lunch at
Salt Grass (hopefully, they will be open!) This may be our
new tradition . . . the Turkey Trot and eating out . . . not the
red-eye from California!

The finale is right around the corner. It's been quite the
journey you all have traveled with us on . . . and we couldn't
have made it without you! I think it's really far from being
over for Abby, and although I told several of you that once you
were on "the List," you couldn't Unsubscribe, even though
it may be hard to give up this captive audience for a mom to
share her love and pride, well . . . I won't hold your e-mail
addresses hostage much longer!

I do pray that Abby will continue to hold your hearts
hostage . . . It's the "plan" she knows has been placed before
her, and we covet your prayers that God's Hand will be in her
every endeavor . . .

With thankful hearts for each of you!

r&b

—e-mail written Sunday, November 22, 2009

The last week in November was a very trying time
when I was struggling with Macy's birthday and the last
few pesky pounds I needed to lose before finale. I was simply sticking to my calorie plan, but the number of hours I
spent working out was not quite as extensive as before. I
was so close to the finish line and losing two, maybe three
pounds a week. As I got smaller and smaller, it became
harder and harder to lose substantial amounts of weight. My
goal for finale was to lose one hundred pounds. Any addi-

tional weight loss would be, as every good Cajun knows, lagniappe . . . the icing on top.

First and foremost, Macy's birthday was Sunday. It kills me . . . every birthday I miss. It's like the grief follows me around and throws a forty-pound blanket over my head and says, "Have fun with this." I stay busy enough not to break down. I probably need a good breakdown, but busy keeps it at bay. I can't allow myself to go to what all I'm missing in her life. It's too painful to go there even for a moment. She would have been nine. Nine. My Macy would have been nine. I miss her . . . in my bones, I ache for her.

Luckily I've had finale looming over my head to serve as a solid distraction . . . Where to begin with my thoughts on finale? I had stayed pretty normal about the whole process until just recently. Now I feel completely overwhelmed, and deep down, in places I don't like to admit even to myself, I feel like a failure. I'm still not at one hundred pounds lost. It's almost like I'm scared to hit that goal. I'm even more terrified of NOT achieving it. I just hope I haven't waited too long to make it happen. I've stayed the course since I've gotten home. I'm not sure what I would have done differently. Maybe I could have been more careful with my calories. I stuck to 1200 very consistently though. I could have put a little more time in the gym . . . though I pretty much gave what I had to give at any certain time.

What's my fear? Disappointing or failing people. How would I respond to that if I was dealing with someone else? I would tell them they had NOTHING to prove to anyone. I would tell them how amazing it is to lose

*ninety-five pounds in six months. So what if you don't lose
another pound. Will you be a different person or be defined by
the number on a scale? No.*

247 didn't define me, and 145 won't either.

—*written in Abby's journal on December 1, 2009*

Before I knew it, it was December and I left for Los
Angeles a few pounds shy of my one-hundred-pound weight-
loss goal, knowing it was going to be close. Preparing for the
live finale at practice, they said each name, the contestant
walked out, and everyone got to lose—you guessed it—one
hundred pounds! Since I was the lightest person, that meant
I won every practice and spent plenty of time standing next
to Alison Sweeney! I told her over and over again, "I just
have to hit one hundred pounds! If I get ninety-nine, I'll be
so disappointed!" Obviously the difference between ninety-
nine and one hundred pounds is insignificant in the grander
scheme of life, but I wanted that moment to be perfect.

The day of the finale was a profound emotional experience; it was the realization of my new normal—the start of
my new life. This pursuit had been the center focus, in the
forefront of my mind for the past seven months, and it was
coming to a close. I was overjoyed that my parents, brother,
nieces, Emily, Tammy, Vicky, Evelyn Addis, and Jeremy
were all there to support me, but I had bittersweet feelings that my family wasn't there to share in the moment.
Clearly, I never would have gone on *The Biggest Loser* if my
family was still alive, but I still missed them terribly and
wanted them with me.

As I walked out onstage, posing in my red finale dress, talking to Alison, and enjoying the fruits of my labor, I savored every second of it. For the quick backstage change, I literally had three minutes to get out of my dress and into my weigh-in clothes; I slipped into place right as they said, "Go!" The cheers from the audience were deafening as I approached the scale. They chanted my name: "Abby! Abby! Abby!" after a video of my story ran on the screen. I watched as the audience stood, bringing me to tears at the sight of a standing ovation. It was just so surreal to be standing for the final time in front of America. When I was tired and fed up with the pressure and the doubts, I would envision standing up on that scale one more time. Now the moment I'd anticipated was here. I watched the numbers roll and then stop. The bright "1," "0," "0" took a second to register: one hundred pounds, on the dot! I was beside myself as the crowd erupted. I heard Julio cheering by Alison and later learned Shay, Rebecca, and Daniel got in trouble backstage for their cheers. The enormous applause masked Alison's request that I say my number aloud. I had no idea she was asking me anything until I saw the tape later at home. Words are inadequate to describe the feeling of pride, the feeling of excitement; it was the culmination of all my hard work. Every part of my journey had materialized into this perfect ending. It was never about winning a title or winning money—it was about winning me! And in that moment I was my own ultimate prize!

Thank you for wanting more information on Abby (or at least making me think you do!!).

She left for Houma last Saturday but will be home for Christmas! Talked with her today and was glad I had waited about finishing my "Abby e-mail."

. . . Abby's dear friend Becky (whom she met through Divine intervention at South Terrebonne High School last year) is helping write her book. She could only entrust her treasured memories and heart with someone she knew loved her . . . and loved her family even though she had never met them! Not sure when it will be completed or published, but we will keep you posted.

Watched It's a Wonderful Life *the other night . . . Oswald Chambers (my all-time earthly hero): ". . . Any problem that comes . . . and there are many . . . while I obey God increases my ecstatic delight, because I know that my Father knows, and I am going to watch and see how He unravels this thing." . . . Also from O.C.: ". . . The author who benefits you most is not the one who tells you something you did not know before, but the one who gives expression to the truth that has been dumbly struggling in you for utterance."*

All this, to say there's a lot of truth we have experienced over the past years that has been "dumbly struggling in us for utterance"!! And It's a Wonderful Life *expresses it so well . . . YOU have made a tremendous impact on our lives while sharing this journey, with your kind messages, with your prayers, with your presence. Our lives wouldn't be the same without you . . . thanks for making it a wonderful life!*

And Merry Christmas!

r&b

—e-mail written Tuesday, December 15, 2009

Soon after the finale, once I settled back into normal life, I went for my first run since finishing with *The Biggest Loser*. It was the best run of my life because it was just for me. I realized, this *is* me. This is what I do. I've made this the new me.

I'm reminded of when I filmed the "Where Are They Now?" episode—to update viewers on my weight loss when my elimination episode aired. Brandon, my story producer, asked me, "Do you wish you were already at goal weight?" I thought about it, and answered, "No, not yet. Because I'm not going to wish away my journey. I don't want to wish away my life anymore." And that is exactly how I feel about my future. Too many times in the past, I thought, *When this happens, I'll be happy.* For the first time since the wreck, I'm happy right where I am; I appreciate the journey.

That doesn't mean that everything is wonderful or that life is easy. I still have to choose every day to continue on, and I still have bad days. My family is still gone, and it is still a struggle. *The Biggest Loser* did not wave a magic fairy wand and declare that I live happily ever after. This is a battle I'll fight forever, but it's a battle I know how to win.

It's hard to break former self-truths that are no longer true. We become slaves to our former selves and habits. The comfort zone is hard to break out of. Though I know I have changed, there is great fear that I might regress. Am I really this fit new person? I have to tell myself every day that this is who I am now. Every time I fit into a smaller pair of pants, I think, *Oh, these must run big.* Every time I run a 5K without stopping, I'm shocked. Will I be able to do it again? Now that I've run more than three miles five times, I'm starting to believe, *Hey wait, maybe this isn't a fluke.* My mind has to catch up with my body.

I was always the smart one. I knew intellectually and academically I would be successful. I had the track record to prove that, but physically—that's a different story. I was always pudgy growing up, not obese, just bigger than the other girls. I might as well have weighed four hundred pounds. I never won a foot race; I was slow and had bad knees. As a perpetual perfectionist, I would rather not participate than not be the best.

I always wanted a quick fix. I wanted a diet pill that made losing weight easy. I seriously contemplated lap band and gastric bypass, wanting the fastest results with the least amount of effort. Isn't that the new American way? But a life truth that has proven itself to me time and time again is that anything worthwhile takes hard work. I have to be aware that I can never become complacent. There are days when I overeat, but I'm learning not to beat myself up over it. There are days when I don't find time to exercise, but that doesn't mean I'm no longer fit. My former truth was that I had to be perfect with my food choices or I was done and shouldn't try at all because I'd failed. That makes as much sense as saying I should drain my bank account because I spent too much on a pair of shoes. This process is not about being perfect. It's about making good choices the majority of the time, knowing that I will make mistakes. I'm human.

I have to get to know myself all over again, and sometimes that scares me. For so long, I secretly had the excuse that whatever bad thing happened, if someone didn't like me or I wasn't hired for a certain job—whatever slight I felt, it was because I was fat. That was my secret truth. Well, those things still happen, and I'm no longer fat. I no longer have that coping mechanism, that built-in excuse. It creates an environment of discomfort. Prolonged periods of discomfort cause us to seek old habits, so I'm learning to find new comforts. It's a daunting task at times, but the payoff is so worth it.

How naïve I was as I embarked on *The Biggest Loser* journey. I needed something different in my life. Deep down I didn't really care about losing weight, I simply wanted to feel better. I wish every overweight person could step into the body of a fit person for one week, maybe just one day. I think it would be the catalyst for a new resolve. If you could "feel" the end, you would stay the course.

For the first time in my life I can run. I don't run fast or far by many people's standards, but I run—something I never dreamed possible. When I run, I am free—mentally and physically free. And every time I run without stopping, I like myself a little more. The truth is I'm still slow, and I still have bad knees. I'm also one of the bigger girls in workout classes and among my friends. The difference is now I have a new measuring stick. Now I have enough physical accomplishments to know that I can be successful in this arena, too. I have to work hard for it; it doesn't come easy, but it's possible.

My paradigm has shifted. Just as the butterfly embarks

on a completely new life, unrecognizable to its former self, flying through the sky instead of crawling along the earth, viewing the world in a completely different way; so does being fit open up a whole new world, a world unknown to the overweight person. I'm shattering my own glass ceiling every day, opening up a world of possibility.

No, in all these things we are more than conquerors through Him who loved us.

Romans 8:37

CHAPTER 13

I Don't Know Much, but I Do Know This— A Letter to the Reader

Any problem that comes...and there are many...while I obey God increases my ecstatic delight, because I know that my Father knows, and I am going to watch and see how He unravels this thing.

— *Oswald Chambers*

As I look back over my journey from October 13, 2006, to the present day, I marvel at what God has done in my life. Of all the challenges I've withstood through His grace, the most significant is still that quiet, unassuming Friday when a split-second swerve across a center line took my entire family. The truth is I still have days when I question, "How will I survive this?" I still have days when I feel like I'm spiraling out of control, and maybe I always will. But the choice I made that evening on the side of the road is the same choice I continue to make daily. I refuse to be a victim, and by choosing to live and respond positively, I am able to live the life God designed for me.

One of the lessons I learned during my time at *The Biggest Loser* ranch was I am much stronger than I knew. Before going on the show, I had reached my "rock bottom." Grief had consumed me to the point where I had, for all practical purposes, given up. I wasn't taking care of myself. I was doing what I had to to exist and little else; however, deep inside I knew I desperately wanted more. Despite having lost the most important people in my life, there was a nagging feeling that I must move forward in this life of mine. I couldn't control how I felt, but I decided that taking care of myself physically might help in the healing process.

Often when you're in that place where you feel like there's nowhere to go, when you've hit your rock bottom, you're more than likely not going to *feel* like doing anything. Finding the powerful person within you requires more than feeling. Sometimes you can't wait until you *want* to make a change; sometimes you just have to do it, and the feelings follow. More often than not, action precedes feeling. I wanted to feel better, but it's not enough to simply want more. I couldn't keep eating ice cream sitting on my couch. I couldn't hide out in my house and wish my life would be better. I had to take action!

I didn't realize I'd have as much healing as I did through physical fitness, but I never knew how to fix the grief. Had I known how to make myself feel better, I'd have done it. I *did* know that there were very tangible, step-by-step things to do to feel better physically. That was something I could control, and when you're that desperate, you'll do whatever it takes. You can't sit back and be a victim, thinking that if only everyone around you changed, life would be perfect. If you don't like your circumstances, you are the common denominator in *your* life. It's about you changing *your* perception. If things aren't going the way you like, then do something about it.

A major part of the process of getting healthy and losing weight is owning up to what you are doing and taking responsibility for your actions. You have to get real with yourself about what you are eating and why you are eating it. Get real with yourself about the intensity of your workouts or the excuses you make for not working out. While facing and telling the truth may be hard in the moment, it makes life easier in the long run. It's not about feeling bad about yourself or making it a sensitive issue. Simply come to grips with the fact that if you're overweight, you're not hiding it. It's not a secret. People know. You're not kidding anyone. When you're ready to get real, you'll start telling people your actual number and stand in "naked clothes" and really look at yourself. Otherwise, you're in denial about the reality of your life.

A weight-loss journey is about so much more than losing physical weight. In order to become truly healthy, in all areas of your life, you are changed. It's not that you change your personality; you do however become the best version of yourself. You get to know yourself on a deeper level by shedding former self-truths and ultimately creating new ones. On some level, everyone wanting to get healthy and make a life change wants more from life, but in order to get a different result, we have to do something different. The dreaded "change" word. Change is scary, but ask yourself this, "If I had to live the rest of my life just as I am now, would I have lived a full life?" If your answer is "No," then *not* changing is far scarier.

Have you put off taking classes at the gym because you think you can't keep up or people might stare at you? Take a deep breath, get there a little early so you can find a comfortable spot, and do your best. Who cares if you can't complete the whole routine? You are doing more than you would be doing had you stayed home fretting about whether or not you were going to go to the class. Don't let fear hold you back! Are you afraid of failing? You've tried to get healthy before, lost the weight, then gained it back? So what! Today is a new day. Some days are harder than others, and you may slide back down the mountain you're trying to climb, but you are not a victim. Do not resign yourself that this is your lot. You're not stuck until you quit. It's not hopeless until you stop trying.

True happiness is, in fact, in the trying. Real joy is in the journey. This journey is not about becoming thin and magically feeling happy. I could have pushed myself to the brink of insanity to lose another ten or fifteen pounds before finale, but losing those pounds would not have brought additional happiness. This journey is about admitting those deep-seated fears, facing them, and learning to love yourself where you are now and where you are going. The prizes I won from *The Biggest Loser* are the relationships I developed, the healthy habits I adopted, and the flare for life I reignited within myself. Creating the balance that was missing from my life trumps the weight loss.

I did not go on *The Biggest Loser* and bare my soul to come back and stay home, count calories, cook every meal, and let food take over my life. I did not go on *The Biggest Loser* for exercise to become my life. I did it to get my real life back, and in any normal authentic life, balance is key.

As humans, our physical, emotional, and spiritual beings must work in conjunction with each other. When one component is out of balance, the others suffer. In the same vein, when an element that has been lacking is improved (physical health), others can improve as well (emotional health). My emotional well-being was thrust to the forefront during my stint at *The Biggest Loser* ranch. Unable to do much physically because of my injury, I was forced to rely on other people for help. I learned the hard lesson that, although we do need to be self-sufficient and ultimately take care of ourselves, human beings need one another. I had to come to terms with the fact that I cannot face the world alone. Yes, I have to do life's work on my own; I can't just sit back and expect people to come in and save me, but it doesn't make me weak to say, "I need you." Once I realized the importance of opening myself up to new relationships, God placed the right people in my life.

An equally important lesson for me was finding a healthy balance with nutrition and exercise. After finale, there was a period when I needed to sit back and enjoy a good "Ahh-hhhhh." Still, I wasted no time in wondering, *Can I really do this?* I'd been hungry for so long. It was the holidays and there was no accountability, a notion that I found radically frightening. My response was to work out regularly and make healthy choices. With the passage of Christmas and into the next few months, I'd gained no weight, fluctuating normally between 151 pounds and 146 pounds. I had to realize that just as I didn't magically lose one hundred pounds in one day, I was not going to wake up one morning and gain one hundred pounds. Weight comes on one and two and three pounds at a time, so when I notice a small gain, I take action.

I am proud of myself and my accomplishments, which helps me to remember that I never want to go back. If that means I count calories for the rest of my life, watch what I eat every day of my life, and say no to things, it's worth it. It's so worth it to feel as good as I do. That doesn't mean that I haven't exceeded my calories for the day on certain occasions.

While traveling with Fresh Grounded Faith, a women's ministry founded by Jennifer Rothschild, I was welcomed into a gracious woman's home who prepared an absolutely lovely meal on gorgeous china. Estimating that, from start to finish, the meal consisted of at least 2,000 to 2,500 calories, I made the conscious decision that I was going to enjoy the dinner and the moment. Running the numbers in my head, I figured out how much I'd need to scale back in the coming days and planned to work out as well to negate any damage I was about to do. Sometimes calories are worth it and sometimes they're not. That night, the experience was *so* worth it.

It's absurd to think that I'm never going to eat what everybody else is eating, indulge in a dinner out, or enjoy a piece of cheesecake with chocolate syrup and a brownie. I am not a failure if I eat a piece a cheesecake; it doesn't mean I'm bad or weak. But I also know that I'm not going to have it every day. I won't indulge every meal. My maintenance stage has been a lifestyle change, finding balance. I never allow myself to feel like I've fallen off the wagon. In the past, I always thought if I ate something high calorie, I was ruined and may as well blow the rest of the day. I'd failed and was a terrible person. That was the inner dialogue I listened to daily. Now, I'm in control, and I have the knowledge I need to make my maintenance stage a way of life.

Getting healthy was always my focus. I'm still not the "skinny girl," but I'm at a comfortable weight I can maintain. I choose not to fall into the trap of thinking no matter how much weight I lose, it's never good enough. Reaching for an elusive state of perfection holds us back from the joy that comes when we're satisfied with the journey we're on. It's important to gain some perspective and realize that everyone has their own issues. By having a positive attitude, you begin to love yourself and your life.

Truthfully, the whole world is hurting, and for some reason, we want to know that we are not alone. When we hear of other people's struggles, sometimes we reexamine our own lives and realize it's not so bad. True happiness comes not from having a perfect life but by simply wanting what you have. We live in a society that tells us to never be satisfied, to always want more. To be content or at peace is perceived as settling. Surely, you can't think that your house, if not a mansion, is good enough. Surely, your older model car is not good enough. This continual state of discomfort leaves us stressed out, apprehensive, tired, and unhappy. We have this perception that we, along with everything around us, has to be perfect. What if you had the power to change that, and it didn't cost a thing? Being good enough where you are is the greatest gift you can give yourself. That doesn't mean you excuse bad behavior or fail to strive to grow. It merely means you don't become paralyzed by the fear of failing and never start the catalyst for change.

Life is an ongoing process in which we are forced to continually face our fears, and we have a choice. We can ignore our fears and allow them to control us, or we can face them and ultimately overcome. Currently I have numerous fears: fear of my ability to maintain my healthy lifestyle, fear of the uncertainty of the future, fear of endless changes. Four years ago, I was in a comfortable spot. I had a plan. I was confident in my abilities, and failure was never a real thought. How I wish I had a formula for eliminating apprehension. But life isn't easy. You may have been feeling the fear as of late, but today choose to face those fears. Today, ask yourself, "What do I have to lose by trying something new?" Today trust yourself enough to take a chance.

I realize now that the weight war is a battle I'll fight forever. It's a part of this new person and this new life I've created. I'm getting to know myself all over again—as a thirty-six-year-old single person, as a fit person. I realize that when you're 247 or 350 or 476 pounds, you feel hopeless, like you'll never see the finish line. But I'm living proof that it's possible. I won't deny that I'm overjoyed to be on this side of the journey. It's been a hard-fought battle, but one that opened up a whole new world for me. The freedom and power I feel when I go for a run, finish a class, or do a personal training session make me believe that I can do it all. Those are triumphs that no one can take away from me. You can't put a price on waking up and having energy! It has not come easily, but I like the person who can run, the woman who can lift weights, the workout buddy who can hike up a mountain, the daughter who can walk around New York with her mother. That résumé makes me proud.

With ability comes responsibility. I now have no excuses. I can do anything I choose to do. My possibilities are limitless, and that scares me sometimes. The world has indeed opened, and it's a big, big world. There are times when I'm juggling speaking engagements or other projects and I'm angry because I know Rick would have handled all this so well. Rick, with his wonderfully organized lists and spreadsheets, could have managed my engagements effortlessly. But he's not here, and I have to handle it.

Some pains never go away. The grieving process doesn't end. People still want to hear that I'm all better, instead of the reality that I still miss my husband and children. The difference is that with my renewed body, mind, and spirit, I can find joy in the small things. It's not such an effort to find things to look forward to. I'm realistic enough to know that I'll have days when I want to curl up in bed and cry. But I won't feel that way every day! I'll take the great days and cling to those, knowing there will be more and more great days to come.

I recently attended my niece's basketball game; it was my first time back in Canton, Texas, in years. I recognized the mother of a little girl named Scarlett, who'd been in Macy's kindergarten class. As her mother and I hugged and began to catch up, Scarlett came bounding up in her basketball uniform—a big green bow in her hair. Nine years old and in the third grade, Scarlett's eyes lit up when she saw me, and she exclaimed, "You're Macy's mom!" My heart skipped a beat at the mention of that treasured title, and I instinctively smiled at her and said, "Yes. I am."

My present-tense response was a reflection of a special progression within my mind. I only just began thinking of Macy as nine years old instead of five. When I recall Caleb's face, I picture a three-year-old, not an infant. Identifying my children with the age they should be helps me to take them with me as I grow older, for I'll always be Macy and Caleb's mom. I am comforted by the memories and the knowledge that they rest in God's kingdom, in a perfect paradise.

I'm not super religious by any stretch, and I sin on a regular, well...daily basis. I certainly do not presume to preach to anyone about how they should live their lives.

Still I feel like I am firmly grounded in my faith. I believe in Jesus Christ as my personal Lord and Savior. I believe in the virgin birth, and that He died on the cross for my sins and rose three days later. I asked Him to come into my heart and forgive me of my sins, and as simple or even trite as that may sound, it saves me from hell. Yes, I believe in heaven and hell, and as unpopular and politically incorrect as it is, I believe that not everyone is going to heaven. I don't believe this because I think I'm better than anyone or that other people are bad. I believe this because it tells me in the Bible. I think that our true purpose on earth is to tell others about Jesus so they get to go, too.

"If it sounds too good to be true, it probably is"—a saying that rings true in our world, except with Jesus. Accepting Jesus is the one thing that is better than what it sounds like. That doesn't mean that your earthly life will be better because you believe in Jesus. In fact, it may be harder. A whole movement of evangelists and preachers who promise health, wealth, and wisdom if only you believe has become so popular in recent years. But the Bible never promises any of that. Ecclesiastes talks about how good things happen to good people, bad things happen to bad people, good things happen to bad people, and bad things happen to good people. Basically, it teaches that life really doesn't make sense.

Jesus endured the most incredibly excruciating, horrible death fathomable. He was betrayed by His closest friends. He was beaten and chastised and spit on, then nailed to a cross. Who are we to think that life is going to be easy for us? Jesus had all the emotions we have. Jesus got angry. He flipped tables in the temple. Jesus wept. He felt sadness just like us. Who are we to think that as long as we are good Christians, only good things will happen to us? Life is a struggle; there is never a time in the Bible where it says, "Follow me and life will be perfect." However, the Bible *does* promise that God will see us through the hard times.

I am still a sinner, but lucky for me, God still loves me. I am sickened by the way the media locks on to the most hateful, angry, mean-spirited people claiming to be "born-again" Christians. These "Christians" are worse than the people they point fingers at and chastise. My God is Love. My God loves everyone. He may hate our sin, but He loves us, unconditionally.

There are many things I can't explain: war, genocide, poverty, my family being taken away from me. But I'm not God, thank goodness for all of you, and I don't have the mind of God. That's where my faith comes in. Even though I hurt and struggle, when I get still enough to listen, I have a peace that really passes all human understanding. You may be reading this thinking I'm absolutely crazy. You may not read any more because I've offended or angered you. But what if there is even the slightest possibility of heaven and hell? Hell—that place where you burn for eternity. Even if there is a chance it exists, wouldn't you want to do anything to avoid going? Even if you accept Jesus under those circumstances, He will begin to reveal Himself to you, and quite frankly, He's cool. You're thinking about it, aren't you? That's the Holy Spirit working on you, but don't wait. The short time we spend on this earth—be it sixty years, eighty years, one hundred years, or two and a half weeks—doesn't really compare to forever. The only promise I can make you with absolute certainty is that your afterlife will be perfect, better than I can describe, better than I can conjure in my simple mind. That I know for sure.

People ask me, "How did you survive? How did you get up again?" The truth is that it is only through God's grace that I press forward. I choose to accept His love and strength and hope that He is able to use this terrible tragedy for good. After the crash, I could have wallowed in self-pity. I could have been mad at God, mad at the man who did this, or just mad at the world in general. Many people have even told me they wouldn't blame me if I did. But hatred, anger, and bitterness are not going to bring my family back. Feeling sorry for myself is not going to make my life count. If I had chosen to go down that path, I may as well have been in the van.

Each and every person reading these pages is doing so because you are supposed to be reading these pages at this exact moment in your life. You need to know you are empowered by your ability to choose. You are not defined by past mistakes. Waste not another moment beating yourself up about the past. Feeling guilty serves no purpose. Today is a new day. You do not have to be defined by past mistakes because I will tell you, just like I would tell the man who killed my family had he survived: today is your second chance to choose differently! We can't control what happens in our lives, but we can control our response. How many times does life take a much different path than the one we planned for ourselves? How many times in life do we let our circumstances dictate our response? Hard times, loss, tragedy, and basic unhappiness are rampant during the course of our lives and can be used as an excuse to give up, but even in light of terrible circumstances, you can *choose* a positive response.

The fact is that life is hard and many times not fair. When things are hard, it's easy to think you will always feel sad or you'll never be happy again. But I'm here to tell you, even in your darkest hour, there is always hope! I am living proof of that. You have the power inside you to be anything you are willing to work hard enough to be. You don't have to be defined by your circumstances. You don't have to be angry and misunderstood. You don't have to feel all alone. Regardless of what other people may have said to you, or even the things you say to yourself, you are fearfully and wonderfully made! You are here for a reason and a purpose. You are worthy of joy and peace!

The beauty of my *Biggest Loser* journey is not that I've gone from a size 20 to a size 6. The beauty of my journey is the healing I have had from the inside out. The outside is really just a reflection of that healing. Living life to the fullest was my heart's desire, and I can honestly say that's what I'm doing: living. As I was driving down the road the other day with the top down on my car, maybe dancing a little, I thought, *I'm happy today.* Though I will never be the same person I was October 12, 2006, I am so much better than I ever thought possible on October 13, 2006. You, too, can be better than you ever thought possible!

ACKNOWLEDGMENTS

A book does not magically happen overnight, as I have learned...I've procrastinated as long as possible in writing this acknowledgments page. I do that... procrastinate when I fear something won't be perfect. I have this horrible thought that I will forget to include someone that has meant much to me in my life, and then the book will be printed, and I won't be able to go back and fix it. Throwing caution to the wind, I will simply write with my heart...

Thanks be to God first and foremost. His grace has been sufficient in my weakness, and He has blessed me beyond measure.

I would not be the person I am today without the example of my parents, Ron and Billie Day. Thank you for your authentic walk with Christ. Thank you for supporting me in EVERY endeavor of my life (from basketball games to school plays—those I was in as well as those I directed—to debate tournaments to being willing to be on camera for *The Biggest Loser*). Thank you for loving my family as much as I did.

Thanks to my brother, Daren Day. The man, father, and husband you are make me so very proud to call you not only my brother, but one of my dearest friends. You and Emily have the kind of love shared by only a fortunate few. That makes my heart über (a word used frequently by my Rick) happy! Emily, you complete our family in such a beautiful way.

Precious Madelyn and Maryl, obviously God has big plans in store for both of you as well. My prayer is you will lean on the Lord and He will grant you the wisdom you need throughout your lives.

Thanks to Becky Prestidge along with her precious husband, Corbin, and two beautiful boys, Noah and Ben. This book would have never happened without your patience, empathy, brilliance, and love. Words are inadequate to adequately thank you for honoring and "getting" my family as though you had known them for years.

Thanks to my cousin, Matt Hoover, for providing me a couch any time I needed! You are one of my favorite people on the planet! Thank you for all the laughter and being willing to listen even after long trips and no special favors.

Thanks to Cindy Matherne for being my friend for all these years and your willingness to read and reread pages and pages of this book. If only the world had more people like you...

Special thanks to Drs. Patrick and Amy Proffer, along with their incredible children, Jake, Allie, Josh, and Ainslee. Thank you also to Karen and Coby Kreigshauser and the rest of the Amarillo gang. You have loved me like fam-

ily and enhanced my life in ways you will probably never know.

Thanks to Christine Batey for loving my nieces like your own children and providing them an incredible example of a Christian woman and the kind of mother others should strive to be.

Thank you to J. D. Roth, Mark Koups, Todd Lubin, Jill Carmen, Kat Elmore, Alison Sweeney, Jillian Michaels, Bob Harper, Dr. H, Sandy Krum, Ashley Sandberg, Allison Katz, Brandon Nickens, Holland Striplin, Ian, Amy, Jackie, Roy, Anthony, Kristen, and the rest of the behind-the-scenes gang, along with all the audio and sound guys at *The Biggest Loser*. What a wild ride...Thank you for the opportunity to change my life for the better.

Thanks to the Tom Landry Center in Dallas, TX, and the Workout Co. in Houma, LA, for providing me a gym family to keep the journey going...The facilities and classes are amazing, but the people make the gym! Thank you to my trainers, Marc Danos and Jeremy Allen, for pushing me to be all I didn't know I could be.

Thank you to Scott Waxman, my literary agent, for your persistence and belief in this project. Special thanks to Lindsey Kennedy for being a calming voice of reason and "getting" me. Thanks to Hachette and FaithWords for helping God turn a horrible tragedy into something beautiful.

And as crazy as it may sound, thank you to the Facebook creators. Thank you for creating a place where people around the world have been able to reach out to me and help me rejoin this wonderful world in which we live. The letters, messages, and wall posts lift my spirits on a daily basis.

Last but certainly not least, thanks to my extended family, dear friends, and former students who have enriched my life beyond measure. Your prayers, support, letters, love, and time have helped me through the good times and the bad. Thank you for being a part of this life of mine.

APPENDIX

LETTERS FROM ABBY AND RICK

—*Rick Rike, written to Abby on their first date*

—*Rick Rike to Abby, May 2003*

May 22, 2003

Okay...so you've just left my house and it's 2:30 in the morning...And I'm writing this knowing I won't give this to you for quite some time...

I guess what it boils down to is you piqued my interest with the infamous ballet. Then I had the absolute BEST first date of my life on Thursday...two weeks ago...I realized then that you were the kind of man that I could love. I didn't think that would ever happen so that was really exciting! Then we kept spending time together and having all those incredible talks. And the more I know of you the more I realize I am falling head over heels for you.

I know people throw the love word around without much thought to what that really means. I take it so very seriously. Love is way more than a passing feeling. It's about mutual respect and caring enough about someone else to put their needs above your own...because you KNOW they want your needs to be met as well. It is the place where you feel safe to be yourself, and where you want to be regardless of the type of day you've had. Love is patient, kind, not jealous or boastful...Using this as my standard, then without hesitation I can tell you that I love you.

You talk about not knowing if there's one perfect person for everyone, and now I believe there is. I think God created you for me and me for you. You surpass my wildest fantasies.

I think we compliment each other so well. It just works! We just "get" it.

I know it's insane to feel this way after two and a half weeks, but there it is. I'm in it...in it completely.

—*written by Abby on May 22, 2003*

262

Keep your eyes on the stars, but your feet on the ground.

Abby,

I saw this card the other day & it just seemed to fit. Indeed you have done it. You decided to move to Aubrey, you told your folks, you told Mr. C & now you put your house on the market... Wow! you have done it & are doing it... MOVING TO AUBREY!

I am so excited & so sure this is the right thing to do that it is almost scary. The prospect of you & Macy moving here once seemed very farfetched. Now, we are going house shopping Friday! What the heck? I am reminded every day just how lucky I am to have found someone so beautiful, intelligent, kind, & loving as you. AND you act me! Did I mention how great it is that you act me?!

The coming days, weeks, months, & YEARS of late-night talks, family gatherings, UIL Tournaments, inservice days, summer trips to far places, lazy days at home, & Macy games/cheer camps & school milestones are truly exciting to me. (It is never too early for us to begin work on her Valedictorian Address for the Class of 2019 ☺!)

I do so love you Abby Davis. The incredible leap of faith you are taking right, obviously attests to me just how much you love me as well. We have talked about this being more than just an Abby & Rick thing & more than a work thing— It is a God thing in my mind & that makes me überHappy! You are truly an incredible person & on top of everything else a great friend. The time we have together indeed does fly by at warp speed, but I enjoy each & every second of it! I am excited about the coming days as we continue down this path of happiness!

I love you,
R²

Abby,

This card is so simple & so understated, yet so perfect. One of my favorite posters is the Jesus Footprints story & this reminded me of it a bit. When I look at the wandering footprints of my life, I have no clue how I was fortunate enough to come face to face w/ you in Austin, TX six weeks ago. And now, we are going to walk side by-side for many weeks, months, & YEARS to come. How exciting is that? I am so glad we met indeed. I am also thrilled, blessed, fortunate, & thankful that we met. You truly are the love of my life. Everyone I have known to this point of my life pales in comparison to you Abby Davis.

You have an incredible last seven days. To think that this last Friday Mr. Mulkey & Tonic were calling me to see if you would consider moving to Aubrey!

Now you are leaving Canton, selling your house, looking at new houses, accepting a new job & GETTING MARRIED! Wow! And it all seems so incredibly natural,

so glad we met.

I am so looking forward to this entire weekend, the rest of this summer, & indeed our lives together! I love you
VERY much,
Abby!

R²

—Rick Rike, from a card depicting two footprints in the sand

Dear Rick,

WOW! I can't believe it is actually happening... married... that is us. You are the man I've prayed for since I was eight years old. You are notorious for all your "stories," so I guess that explains why I'm getting to experience the greatest love story of all time! What a story it makes! More importantly, what a great life it makes!!!

You amaze me everyday. It's hard to believe that I am able to love you more now than I did six weeks ago and to firmly know I will love you even more a year from now... ten years from now... fifty years from now...

I know we've talked about it before, but I truly would go through every part of my life and not change a thing so that I could be at this point in my life with you. I didn't know it, but you were the thing missing in my life. You are my split apart, and I thank God every day for you. It's hard to remember life before you because I feel like I have known you forever... luckily I get to spend forever with you.

Thank you for being the man you are... honorable and sensitive and kind and passionate and creative and humble and everything I could want in a mate and more. My cup runneth over! →

I love and honor and adore you, and I promise I will live my life so that one day you can say, "I've had a great life!"

Ashly Rike

Dearest Rick,

It's hard to believe we've been married a month! It's even harder to believe how much my life has changed since I met you such a short time ago. You have brought such joy to my life! Thank you!

As I reflect back over the journey that brought me to this place, I really do have never loved a man until you. You are everything a husband should be... kind, patient, giving, willing to talk things through, romantic, affectionate, and a true leader! Thank you!

"You" wow me on a daily basis. My Macy has now become our Macy. I don't know if I ever thought I could share her rearing with anyone, but you make it so easy. You touch my heart everytime you read to her or give her a bath or tell her bedtime stories. You are such an incredible dad! You love her even when she's being somewhat unloveable. That takes a very strong man. Thank you!

If this month is indicative of the next fifty years then I will have lived a blessed life. It is my prayer that I will be the kind of wife you need and deserve for the next fifty years. Our foundation is strong and our future

us so bright! Together we can face anything. Thank you for making me a part of the greatest love story of all time. I can't promise that it will always be easy facing the challenges of life, but I can promise that I will love, honor, respect, adore, and cherish you til death do us part!

I do so love you, Rick!

APPENDIX

My dearest Rick,

So I'm hoping this will look original, this whole writing in a folder thing, rather than I've had no time to get you the "perfect" card... But then again, that is what makes US so special!

I'm almost overwhelmed tonight by how much I love you. You absolutely amaze me. You make me feel so loved and appreciated. There is no man on this earth that could ever compare to you. When I was at my lowest point several years ago, and I cried out to God to send me a Godly, manly-man that was sensitive and kind and good, I had no idea she would surpass my wildest fantasies with you. I love everything about you... from the way you love Macy, to the way I feel safe in your arms... from the way you are the ultimate optimist to the way you can fall asleep faster than any human I've ever known... a sign of the clearest conscience!! You are the perfect man for me.

This year has definitely been a challenge, and I am so sorry for all the times I've been selfish thinking it was harder for me. It is such a small price to pay to get to wake up in your arms each day. Please forgive that selfishness, I will be better.

This is your year to shine professionally. I want you to savor every second of your success because you deserve it! There will be no one more proud for you and of you when you get your first UIL state champion's ring this year. I must admit a small (or maybe large) part of me is thrilled to get to share that with you.

I have a great feeling about this weekend. Don't underestimate for one second what an amazing coach you are. If anyone is the Pied Piper, it is you. You inspire everyone around you to live their personal best... that includes kids, adults, and luckily for me, me! Thank you for being the role model you are!

You are the man of my dreams and the greatest love of my life. I thank God every day for you. And as a very wise man once said... if these seven months are any indication of how our lives will be, then we are the luckiest people on earth.

I do so love and adore you,
Wallace Richard Rike!
Abby

—written inside of a manila folder

Abigail,   19 May 2004

Where has the time gone dear wife of mine? Was it really ten months ago today we were under the Glad Oak? That day was very special & one I still think about every day of my life. The best decision I ever made was getting married to you & Macy. The last three hundred days have been the happiest of my life. The joy you bring on a daily basis surpass anything I ever dreamt possible. I thank God every day that we have our time together. Time is something that is so easy to take for granted. The fact is we have no clue how long we have together. We might have sixty minutes, sixty days or sixty months together. I hope we have sixty years ahead of us to watch Macy grow up, build our dream house together, win state championships, & grow closer & closer together. The fact is I cherish all of our days, our nights & our conversations together. Never have I cared for anyone or anything like I care for our family. The comfort that comes from knowing we will spend eternity together is wonderful. Of course there will be times in our lives when

time flies or we get busy or we are less attentive, but my prayer is those times are fleeting. The fact is I truly believe we just endured the toughest four & a half months we will ever face together. Not only leaving here, but leaving so many obligations behind will pave the way to much easier times in future years. Never again will we have the challenges we had this year. Never again will we people trying to undermine who we are & what we do. As I have said time & again, the fact we could survive this semester & this year speaks volumes to who we are & what we have. If we could bottle this up & sell it, we would have our millions we want! :)

I am so anxious to get out of Tioga, to get out of Aubrey, & to get on with our lives. The future indeed seems so very bright. This summer will be great, next year at Canton will be wonderful - certainly not perfect as that isn't realistic - but wonderful. I look forward to working for & with YOUR people. I have all the confidence that will work out & we will have a great time together.

Another way I know just how much I love you is because of the fact I am not stressing about my work future. I love you so much that I really don't care if I am a Wal Mart greeter or a mechanic or a high school computer teacher. I simply want to spend time with you, love you, dote on you, kiss you, talk to you, share my life with you, & grow old with you. Everything else is trivial at this point. We are going to quickly put this year & our experience here to rest. Never again will we have to endure what you & we have endured this year. I am thankful each day that you have & do love me enough to forgive my mistakes & endure this year. Soon we will be able to enjoy normal life in Mabank & if life gets better than this, I am one LUCKY man! Thank you for the greatest ten months of marriage ever!

I love you!

R²

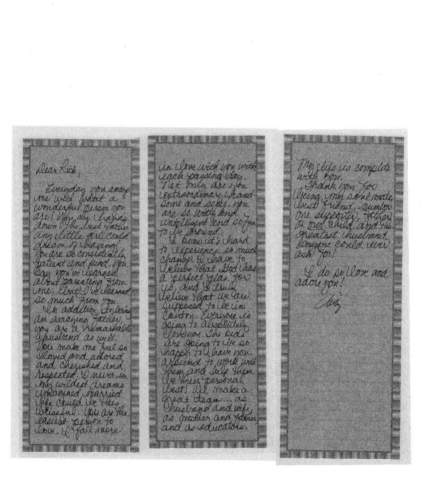

6 June 2004

Little Macy,

What a big day Monday is going to be! Your FIRST day of gymnastics class. I hope you know how incredibly proud your mother and I are of you. You are the most intelligent, sweetest, loving, and most beautiful child in the world. You are such a joy to have in my life. You are everything every daddy could ever need or want in a daughter. You have accepted me with open arms over the past year and I will forever be indebted to you for that. Thank you so much for accepting me into your family. Now the Rike family is growing and maturing together. I am so excited about not only your gym class, but other things going on in our lives. We are also going to be taking one step closer to other things after today. There will be a day later in your life when you are an all star gymnast that everyone is reading about in the newspaper....they will say, "Wow—that Macy Marie Rike is really something. She is a great Texan, a great American, and a great daughter. Her parents sure must be proud of her." And you know what—they will be right. The thing is there is no doubt about the fact you are a winner. Whether you choose gym or sports or academics or politics or band or whatever—you are going to be successful. And....no matter what, we will always be proud of you. You just have to remember to be determined, be patient, be kind, and above all else....NEVER give up. You are an amazing little girl and we are the luckiest parents in the world because we get to watch you grow up everyday!

I love you with all my heart,
R^2
Daddy

Abigail Denise,

Wow! What a unique Valentine's Day this is. We are pregnant ☺ I never imagined I could be this happy over having a little Ribeling on the way! Wow! We are pregnant! Our love is truly a unique thing I know. We are so lucky to have the love that we have. Most people look forward to V-Day because it is one of the few days of the year where they feel loved. Lucky for me, I feel loved every day of the year. You do an incredible job of making sure I feel loved in so many ways. I love the way you scratch my back when I most need it. I love the way you look at me w/ adoring eyes. I love the way you let me know you think I am a good husband. I love the way you let me be a true father to Macy. I love the way you go so far to show me you do care about my interest, whether it is sports, politics, or whatever, I know you truly do care just because you know it is important at that moment to me. And... I love the way you are so excited about having our baby! I am so thrilled!!

My resolution for the coming year is to be more & more thoughtful. I feel like I have good spells & than dry spells. Sometimes I do well & there are still periods where I do not consider your needs enough. You are the absolute perfect wife for me... & I am going to continue to strive to be the perfect husband to you. This new edition to our family is indeed going to change things – that is a given. I have no doubt at all that this is going to continue the greatest period of my life. For someone who was never going to have kids, I sure have done a 180° – Now maybe we should have four or five more ... well maybe not ☺ – But I have every confidence that I am going to love raising our children together. You are the perfect mother to Macy. I am going to have to learn from you again about this whole infant parenting – I am so looking forward to it. You are truly an amazing wife, mother, best friend, parenting buddy & Valentine.

I have you a little present in the freezer ☺!

Top Seven Things That are likely to change with the arrival of Reagan/Austin/Lauren Elisabeth D.D. Rike:

7. Wal-Mart trips for pictures of TWO!
6. Macy starts to crave "alone time"
5. More manly shampoos appear in our shower.
4. UIL slides down another notch in importance.
3. Mack who? (at least for Fall 2006 ☺)
2. My sleeping patterns.

1. MY phobia of dirty diapers!

One thing that will never change: My never-ending love for

YOU!

I love you - R²

Dearest Rick,

You truly are the most amazing man I have ever known. Somehow you make me fall more in love with you with each passing day. (I have loved you with every ounce of my being practically since I have known you... I guess my capacity to love has increased.)

Watching you with Macy touches me to my core. You are so kind and patient and loving and thoughtful and stable with her. When I watch her run to hug you or snuggle up next to you I am reminded just how lucky we are. You make our lives complete.

Our family life is so incredible as it is right now, it's hard to imagine it getting even better! I grow more excited everyday

with the thought of bringing our Caleb into the world. God has blessed me far more than I have ever deserved, but I am so very thankful everyday. Our family is the most precious thing to me, and I will work every single day to be the best wife and mother I can be. Thank you for your continued patience and support of me. You inspire me with your example to be the best person I can be.

The upcoming months will be a mixture of enormous change and enormous happiness. I look so forward to sharing this experience with you. Even though it's kind of scary, I know everything will be fine because we are in it together.

I do so love and adore you!

272

Ab,

Just for the record... this spending 9 to 12 hours a day apart from one another is for the birds! I do not like it one little bit. I am so spoiled to us spending all of our time together. There have been far too many evenings of late where I was too tired to function. I know I need to fight through my tiredness & be there more regularly for you & for Mary. You are so good to me & patient with me. You are my hero for carrying Baby Huey- especially these past two months that have been so agonizing.

I truly never imagined marriage could be this good, this easy, this rewarding, this fulfilling? You are truly an amazing woman that makes me feel like the luckiest person on Earth. I have said it before & will say it again- many, many more times. You are perfect for me in so many ways. You bring out the best in me & make me want to be the best husband & father possible. One thing I have come to realize is how much you lift my spirits at school. It has not been until recently that I have been here without you that it has hit me. No matter what went on with kids or whatever at school, it was all okay once I saw you, touched you,

held you, heard from you- and I miss seeing you, touching you, holding you, & hearing from you all throughout the day at school. I never imagined this time apart would be so difficult. I have not always handled it well, I know. I am trying to enjoy the moments we have together more because they should be special right now. My resolution for these final 12 days of pregnancy & the start of Colbie time here with us is to not sweat the small stuff, enjoy & cherish our family, & make sure this is a time we will all look back on with the fondest of memories. Thank you for everything -
I love you & miss you & feel so lucky to have the opportunity to raise our two children together !!

R²

273

10 Oct '06

Abby,

Wow! We have children now. We are responsible adults w/ a minivan, two kids, & a house. Some days I am amazed at where we are. Other days I am just in awe. Other days I feel a bit overwhelmed. But _every_ day I feel fortunate.

Fortunate to be married to you.
Fortunate to shy my days & nights w/you.
Fortunate to have the rest of lives to look forward to together.

...there wouldn't be grateful people like me!

You complete me & you are the most amazing Supermom - EVER! No man could possibly have a better wife, best friend, soulmate, kids, & family life than I do. Thank you for sharing this life w/ me ♡ R?

—*written October 10, 2006, three days before the wreck*